APPALACHIAN HERITAGE

VOL. 46, NO. 2
SPRING 2018

ESTABLISHED IN 1973

PUBLISHED QUARTERLY
by Berea College
CPO 2166
205 N. Main Street
Berea, KY, 40404

www.appalachianheritage.net

 Periodicals postage paid at Berea, Kentucky, and at additional mailing offices. ISSN# 03632318.

Electronic submissions only at www.appalachianheritage.net

Distributed by the University of North Carolina Press. Basic subscription price: $30/year for individuals, $60/year for institutions. For subscription requests and inquiries, visit the magazine's website, email uncpress_journals@unc.edu, or call 919.962.4201.

CONTENTS

INTERVIEW

CRAFT ESSAY

A note on the photograph: Dancers from the "Children of Shangri-Lost" prepare to perform a story of their families' journey from Bhutan to Nepal to Pittsburgh at City of Asylum in the Mexican War Streets on Tuesday, July 5, 2016. From left, Rabina Phuyel, 17, sits as Bandhana Bhattarai, 15, winces while getting her hair braided by Binsha Bhattarai, 15. Continuing right, Ritika Chamlagai, 15, takes a photo of her handiwork on Deepa Phuyel's braids, age 20, and on the bottom right, Hera Nepal, 17, looks on. All the young women now live in Baldwin, Pennsylvania. With around 5,000 people, the Bhutanese community is one of the largest refugee and immigrant communities in Pittsburgh.

EDITOR'S NOTE

JASON HOWARD

Last month my writing group descended on our home in Berea for a weekend of words and kinship. We are a close-knit bunch, with friendships reaching back over a decade and, in some cases, even longer. Our group meets each quarter, and more if we can manage it. We often converge here in Berea, but we have also been known to frequent other locations, including a Kentucky state park and Airbnbs in Nashville and Louisville.

The weekend goes like this: we gather on Friday afternoon, our respective cars loaded with books, laptops, notebooks and libations, and then we visit. Saturday afternoons are usually devoted to workshop, and before we know it Sunday morning has arrived, when we must follow the highways back to our separate lives.

During our time together, we always end up talking, eating, and drinking as much as writing and workshopping. But that's part of the point. Feeding the soul means feeding the craft, and we are quick to exchange all manner of information and recommendations gathered in our time apart. Last month, one of our members spotted a clutch of shockingly blue spider lilies growing in our backyard. She asked my husband for a cutting.

"Sure," he said, and after fetching a knife, they left to retrieve the plant.

Another member observed this and grinned. "She doesn't know what she's asking for. Those things spread like wildfire."

I've thought about that exchange over the past few weeks, turning it over in my mind. It was an aside, one that reflected the ease of friendship among all the involved parties. Once planted, the flowers will be a reminder of that friendship, of our group, of the breezy May morning on which they were cut. But it was the image of the plant I kept landing on, how it might look when it does spread all over her garden. I needed a concise, visceral description for that image, and time after time I came up short.

Community—that's the word I was searching for. A community of flowers, of friends, of words. A term increasingly threatened today by nationalism, tribalism, prejudice, and a frightening lack of attention to language—to words and their consequences—and decorum.

Nowadays, we need literary writing more than ever. We need writers who worry over their words, work that both moves and shakes us.

In this issue, I am pleased to offer such work from two poets who are engaging in this conversation on a national level. Lyrae Van Clief-Stefanon and Rebecca Gayle Howell were the visiting writers at the 2017 Appalachian Symposium, and between them they have contributed poems, an essay, and a powerful conversation from the event itself. Sterling writing also appears from Mary Ellen Miller, Jane Hicks, Lisa J. Parker, Jon Sealy, Pauletta Hansel, and others, serving to create a formidable gathering of spirit, beauty, and entertainment on the page.

Community: a beautiful word. *Commune*, its root. As you read through these offerings, these meditations, take time to commune with our contributors and their words, their characters, their ideas—all the flowers in their literary gardens. May they spread like wildfire. ■

BERRY PATCH

MARY HOSTETTER

It was not so much that Herbert was gone, although she missed him, but how he'd done it, that bothered Irene. Sometimes she could go a whole day and not think about him, at least not to dwell on it. But her brother John insisted on coming over from Richmond for the first anniversary of Herbert's death. John didn't think she should have to go to the cemetery alone. She didn't tell him that if he hadn't come, she wouldn't have gone to the cemetery at all, let alone plant those flowers. Now John had gone home, but his talk about Herbert and questions about why he did it had gotten her mind all spinning again. Did John think after all these months she would suddenly figure out the answer?

She and John planted yellow pansies, the ones with purple centers, next to the gravestone. They were Herbert's favorite flower, and she'd always planted them in the iron bucket on the corner of the porch for him. "They have such happy faces," Herbert had said, which was odd when you think about it, him noticing a flower looking happy.

Irene sat at the kitchen table eating leftovers from the meal she'd made for John the evening before—roast beef, mashed potatoes and lima beans. The house seemed quiet with him gone. Only sound Irene heard was Sweetness at the other end of the table lapping from her bowl.

It had been good to see John again, even with his questions. She hadn't seen him since the holidays when he'd insisted she come over to join him and his family for Christmas. It was what she and Herbert had done in years past. It was hard being around all that holiday excitement, but maybe it was better than being alone.

■ ■ ■

The afternoon before he left, she'd said to John, "I'd like to send something along for Polly and the girls."

"Nothing they like more than your chocolate chip cookies," John said.

As often as she'd made those cookies, it had been a long time, and Irene needed the recipe. She sorted through recipe cards she hadn't looked at in years. And she had to find the measuring spoons. Imagine, not knowing where to find your measuring spoons. She didn't bake like she used to when Herbert was alive.

It was when she was making those cookies, while John made phone calls and got his things together, that she thought about the last time she'd made chocolate chip cookies. She used to make them almost every week to put in Herbert's lunch. They were his favorites. He said store-bought ones weren't nearly as good, and of course they weren't.

There must have been chocolate chip cookies in his lunch box the day he did it. Why did Herbert even take a lunch that day if he knew he wasn't going to eat it? To keep her from running out to the truck after him? Was the lunch bucket still in the truck when they brought it back to her? So many pieces she couldn't put together about that day.

She'd sold the truck, advertised it in *The Penny Saver*. A man from over beyond Charleston called after dinner the day the paper came out.

"Hello, I'm Floyd Ramsey, and I see you have a truck for sale," he'd said. "Can you tell me a little about it?"

"It's a '73, not even three years old," she said, "and never caused any trouble at all." As soon as she said it, she felt bad, like she was lying, which, of course, she wasn't. The fact that the truck killed Herbert didn't mean anything was wrong with the truck.

"Why you looking to get rid of it?"

"It's my husband's. He passed away."

"I'm sorry."

"Thank you."

"You say here you'd like $2500 for it."

"That's right."

"Consider any less?"

"I might," Irene said, even though she wanted to tell him she'd practically give it away if he'd take it out of her sight. "What would you offer?"

"Well, I'd like to come see it. If it's in good shape, I'd give you $2000.

"That seems fair."

The day after Floyd Ramsey called, Irene cleaned out the truck, took out Herbert's toolbox and flannel shirt. She didn't remember ever taking out the lunch box that must have been on the seat beside him that morning, probably right next to the hose. She didn't know what happened to the hose either.

Floyd Ramsey had come over with his son the following weekend, wrote her a check, and made the truck disappear.

■ ■ ■

Irene didn't like all the memories coming back. She'd just as soon have let the anniversary go by without thinking about it, but with John visiting, and making the cookies, things were coming back up.

Irene finished eating the leftovers and shoved the plate across the table so Sweetness could lick up the last of the gravy. She ate a couple of the cookies she'd kept back, the ones that burned on the bottom.

She'd never understand how Herbert could do it, pulling his truck off on the logging road where someone would find him when they went to work, putting a hose on the exhaust. She wondered what he was thinking in those final minutes. It couldn't be quick, that kind of death. She was sure that young man who found him—hadn't even been working at the mill a month—still hadn't gotten over it. She missed Herbert. They'd had good times, especially in the beginning, but wasn't that true for everyone. If only he'd left a note, anything. Got out of bed that morning and said, "I've got to go in a little early to do some bookwork before the men come in," and she had to get the news from a man she hardly knew. How could you make sense of something like that? How had that last morning gone? Did he say, "Bye, Sweetie" or "See you later?" Was she still in the kitchen when he left? Did he give her a quick kiss on the way out, or was she already in the bedroom getting dressed, and he called "Bye" through the door? Maybe it didn't matter, but she would have paid more attention if she'd known it was the last time.

She read everything she could get her hands on, articles in *Reader's Digest*, books from the bookmobile. She must have missed warning signs, but he wasn't withdrawn, hadn't

Irene didn't like all the memories coming back. She'd just as soon have let the anniversary go by without thinking about it...

been giving his things away, didn't talk about not wanting to live. And demons? What kind of demons could he have? Sleeping right next to him, making love to him. Wouldn't she have known if he had demons? She'd been over it forward and backward, looking for what she might have missed. Luther and Phyllis' boys had come over to borrow Herbert's shovel and rake to work the fertilizer into the rows for the berries. Herbert said, "Keep them as long as you'd like." Could that count as giving his things away?

He wasn't a man to talk much, but the marriage couldn't have been that bad without her knowing it. They never had those loud arguments you could hear through the open windows in the summertime from Luther and Phyllis's house next door.

■ ■ ■

Sweetness jumped down from the table and went toward the bedroom. Irene cleared the table, washed the dishes and stacked them in the drainer. She went into the living room and turned on the light next to her chair. Some day she'd get rid of the photos on top of the bookcase, wedding pictures, photos from the cruise they took for their tenth anniversary. All that seemed a long time ago. She kept them there, dusting them each week. Maybe one day she'd put them away, but not yet.

Irene turned the gold wedding band on her finger, pulled it off and put it back on. It still came off easily. Why did she still wear it? Maybe she should have thrown the wedding band in the grave along with Herbert's ashes. She'd thought about it, but would have felt naked not wearing it the day of the funeral. Would she always be a widow? Since she hadn't taken the ring off right away, now she didn't know when the time would be right. Everyone would notice. Of course they would, seeing her every day, and who knows what they'd make of it? It would have made sense if she'd done it right after Herbert died.

■ ■ ■

One evening she'd tried to talk to Herbert, seriously talk, but it was nothing close to an argument. It was the week after they got back from the cruise, and Herbert was sitting across from her at the table. He usually didn't stay around for conversation after dinner, and Irene asked her question while he was still eating dessert, chocolate pudding, the kind that came in the box.

"Don't you care that we don't have children?"

"What kind of question is that?" Herbert said. "We've already talked about it. It would be great."

"But there must be a problem if I never get pregnant. It's been ten years. I read an article in *Reader's Digest,* and doctors can do simple things to see what's wrong and try to fix it. Both of us would have to get checked."

"We're doing what we're doing, and kids will come if they're meant to. If not, we'll do without. No one needs to be checking me out top to bottom. You either."

Herbert got up, pushed his chair in, went into the living room, picked up his *Field and Stream* and turned on the TV.

Irene never brought it up again, and children never came. Herbert was good with kids. She'd seen him with his nieces and nephews, with the boys next door. For a time she'd thought a lot about having kids, but as she got older, she let it go. If they'd had children, could Herbert have done what he did?

■ ■ ■

Irene flipped through the latest *New Yorker.* Nothing caught her attention, which often happened, and she put it aside. She'd add it to the stack along the wall. Sometimes when she wrote to John she'd go through *New Yorkers* and cut out a cartoon to send along. Most of them didn't make much sense to her—she could only think of a few times she found one that was good for him.

She was the only one in town who got the *New Yorker*—a gift subscription from John each year. She might have preferred a different magazine, maybe *Good Housekeeping,* but John knew she liked to read and thought he was giving her something special.

She sorted the mail at the post office and knew what magazines everyone got. She read a lot of them, all she cared to, careful not to turn down the pages and putting them back in the mailboxes when she finished. No one would mind. Not a lot to do sitting there all day waiting for people to come in for their mail, to buy stamps or mail packages. She cleaned the windows, dusted the counter, swept and mopped the floor every day, but that still left lots of time. It was a little post office, not much bigger than a shed.

She'd heard rumors a few years ago that the post office might be closed down, that it wasn't worth a zip code all its own, and the people in Tanner's Gap wrote letters to protest. Irene hadn't written any letters, since she was an employee, but she felt as strongly as the rest of them. What kind of thing is that to tell a town? That they aren't worth their own zip code. It stayed open, and now that Jimmy Carter was president, it didn't seem like they were in danger anymore. Seemed like he understood what small towns needed.

Other than the *New Yorker*, the only magazine Irene subscribed to was *Reader's Digest*, and that stack was in the corner of the living room, halfway up to the window. The stack was lined up straight, and, if you looked quickly, it didn't look as much like a stack of magazines as it did a plant stand, which

She'd thought about moving away after Herbert died, living in a bigger city, like she always planned...

is what she used it for. She'd put the spider plant on it, the one Etta gave her after Herbert did what he did. The plant already had five shoots. Looked like the fireworks on the photo from the cruise ship that set behind the plant. They'd set the fireworks off on the last night.

Irene had seen an article in the newspaper about a woman found dead in her house somewhere in Texas. The floors in her house were covered with trash and clutter so deep she couldn't walk through except for one narrow path. The police who found her said it looked like she hadn't thrown anything out in years. Irene was glad she wasn't like that. She did keep things, but only things that might come in handy, and she didn't leave them strewn around the floor. She liked things neat. No one kept a floor cleaner than she did. Not a week went by she didn't vacuum at least three times, if not more, especially with the cat hair.

And she was organized. Never in the years she worked at the post office had anyone found the wrong mail in their box, and the stamp and postage money came out right every time. Herbert had her help with the books for the mill, and the new supervisor even came to her for help after Herbert was gone.

She'd thought about moving away after Herbert died, living in a bigger city, like she always planned before his lumber company asked him to go to West Virginia to set up the mill. It didn't seem fair to leave. A post office is important, and the town depended on her. When Joyce filled in for her now and then, people said things didn't run as smoothly, and Irene was sure they didn't.

■ ■ ■

After Herbert's funeral, she'd packed up all his clothes, and John took them along to donate to the Goodwill in Richmond. She was glad they went far away; she didn't want to see anyone walking around in one of his checked shirts. Before bagging them up, she looked in every pocket for a note or a clue to why Herbert did it. She didn't expect to find anything but had to look. Herbert was not the sort of man who'd spend a lot of time hiding a note. If he wanted to leave a note, he'd be likely to leave it on the refrigerator door with a magnet, right next to the grocery list, or slipped into the checkbook, a place he knew she'd find it.

A few days after the funeral, she got the idea that Herbert had put a note between the pages of one of the books on the shelves in the living room, and she was determined to find it. At first she tried to keep the books stacked neatly as she took them off the shelves, shaking them by their spines, waiting for a note to fall out. She shook the Bible she'd taken from her mother's bedside table after she died, and a folded piece of paper fluttered out. It almost made her sick imagining that's where Herbert would have chosen to hide his note. When she could finally bring herself to open the folded paper, it was a recipe a friend at church must have given her mother for a three-bean salad. She grabbed the books and shook them so hard that a few pages fell out before she flung them across the living room. She didn't even stop when one of the books almost hit Sweetness, not until all the shelves were empty. She didn't care what it would look like if a neighbor stopped by with food or flowers and saw books strewn all over. She'd gone a little crazy that night, and she hated that Herbert had turned her into that kind of a person.

Some of the articles she read talked about people who committed suicide not seeing any other way to stop the pain. What pain of Herbert's could have been as bad as what he caused her? Some days, especially early on, it felt like shame, but what had she done, or not done, to be ashamed of? For a time it almost felt like people in town tried to avoid her, in case suicide was a disease that could be catching.

She'd written a letter to "Dear Abby," as if that would help. She never mailed it, found it in the desk drawer a couple weeks ago, all typed and folded in an envelope. She read it again, put it back in the drawer.

Dear Abby,
A couple months ago my husband left to go to work one morning, pulled his truck off the side of the road,

hooked a hose up to the exhaust and killed himself. He didn't act any different that I noticed and wasn't going through any stress. Our marriage was good, as far as I could tell. How can I make sense of this? I know he did it to himself, but it feels like he was doing it to me.

Signed,
Angry Widow in West Virginia

People in town read "Dear Abby," and Irene was sure they'd guess it was her letter. Maybe that's why she didn't send it, not knowing how Dear Abby would respond. What if she said that if Irene had noticed the signs, she could have kept it from happening? She didn't need the whole town reading a thing like that.

■ ■ ■

Irene hadn't thought this much about Herbert in months. She had trouble getting to sleep. She'd even turned on the television, just for the company. She swore she'd never do that, acting like those pathetic people who kept their televisions on in the background all day and into the night.

The next morning she got up, fed Sweetness and dressed for work. It wasn't even a half mile down the road to the post office, and she always walked if the weather was nice. The exercise was good. She was sure it helped keep the weight off. She pulled her hair back into the same twist she'd worn for most of her adult life; she didn't look any older than she did twenty years ago. It was important to her to keep her figure, and Herbert had appreciated it too. Lot of good that did her.

Irene filled Sweetness' water bowl, put on her jacket and locked the door on her way out. It was ten years ago when she and Herbert moved into their house. When they first moved to Tanner's Gap, they rented a drafty old farmhouse, and it was a relief to move into the new brick rancher. The house was warm, with good insulation, windows that sealed and everything so airtight it was hard to close the door in winter. They both swore they'd never live in an old house again. With the storm windows down and sheets of plastic taped on the inside, the heating bills weren't much of anything, even in the coldest part of the winter.

Next door Luther and Phyllis lived in a brick rancher too. They had a woodstove in theirs, and, when Irene and Herbert went over, which they often did, Luther and Phyllis's house felt cold. Of course they didn't have plastic on their windows, and the whole winter could go by without them remembering to put the storm windows down. With the boys running in and out, the doors were open all the time.

Irene was relieved no one was outside at Luther and Phyllis's when she walked by. It felt like a different lifetime when they'd spent all that time together.

■ ■ ■

She and Herbert had been over at Luther and Phyllis's for a cookout the Friday before Herbert did it. Phyllis had called before Irene left for work that day.

"Can you believe this weather? It feels like spring."

"I know. All I need to wear is a sweater to walk down to work," Irene said.

"Anyway, Luther wants to have a cookout. And still March, if you can believe it," Phyllis said.

"Great. What can we bring?"

"We've got burgers and rolls, and I'm sure we have ice cream to pull out for dessert. How about you bring beans and a salad?"

"No problem. Herbert will love it. A cookout in March."

They had such fun that evening. Phyllis and Luther's boys had gone camping with their cousins, and it was just the four of them. They stayed outside and watched the sun go down behind the mountain. The men drank a few beers, and Irene and Phyllis had wine.

They all stood beside the empty lot between their houses. Luther had tilled it a few days before, and the boys worked in the fertilizer.

"We'll have space for all kinds of berries," Luther said.

"As long as you have plenty of raspberries," Herbert said, "I'll be happy."

"Where are we going to sell these berries when they get ripe all at once?" Phyllis said.

"I was thinking maybe you girls could make jams and jellies if we get too many at the same time."

"I thought this was the boys' 4-H project," Irene said.

"They could help make the jelly, and they'd need to figure out the marketing part, talk to the people up at Marshall's about selling it at the store, or over at the diner," Luther said.

"Seems like you and Herbert are taking this project over," Phyllis said.

"We need to help them get started," Luther said.

Luther and Herbert spent hours talking about the berry patch. Some evenings Irene saw them out the kitchen window when she was getting dinner, standing by that empty lot, pointing and talking, pounding in stakes, moving them. No question they were excited about it.

Irene hadn't been over to Luther and Phyllis's more than once or twice in the year since Herbert was gone. One of those times was when a wind storm brought down a tree, and one of the branches blocked her from getting the car out of the driveway. She'd gone over to ask Luther and Phyllis' boys to help her move the branch. Almost broke her back trying to do it on her own before she went next door to ask if they'd give her a hand.

■ ■ ■

Irene got to the post office a few minutes early. It was stuffy when she opened the door, but she liked the smell, paper and ink and the lemon polish she used to keep the counter clean. That old counter was the most beautiful piece of cherry she'd ever seen. They said it was over a hundred years old. Herbert always told her you couldn't get a board that wide anymore, cherry especially, and he knew his wood. She put up the blinds, and the sunlight streamed in through the windows she'd cleaned a few days before. You could see the bubbles and ripples in the old glass.

She took the mail that had been dropped in the mail slot, postmarked it and put it in the bag to go out. She'd started sorting the incoming mail, putting it in the boxes, when James Wilcox, the new minister, came in. He came in every day, but this was the first time he was the only customer.

"You're probably not even open yet," he said, "but I was hoping these letters could go out today."

"No problem, I'll stamp them and add them to the bag," Irene said.

"Sure do appreciate it," James said.

"No excuse not to be accommodating with a post office this small," Irene said.

"Thanks."

Irene postmarked his letters, opened the bag and threw them in.

"You know," James said, "I had no idea you'd been through such hard times. I'm sorry about what happened to your husband."

He said it as if it had happened last week and not a year ago. Irene was taken by surprise. No one but her brother mentioned Herbert anymore. It was as if he had never existed.

"Thank you for your sympathy," Irene said.

Maybe Derwood or Etta thought it their Christian duty to give the new minister the lowdown on everyone in town. Maybe someone at church on Sunday gave Irene's name as a prayer request.

"We'd be happy to see you at church again," James said. "People have talked about getting the choir going, maybe for special occasions, if you'd be interested in singing."

"I don't go out much anymore," Irene said.

"I sometimes have to push myself to do things that might be hard at first," James said. "Don't know about you."

"Probably how it is for most of us," Irene said.

After James Wilcox left, Irene went back to sorting the mail. She hadn't put but a few letters in the boxes before Frank Talbert came in.

"Well, good morning. I see James Wilcox was already paying you a visit. There would be a catch for you. Not every day a single man in his prime makes it all the way across these hills."

"Things are just fine the way they are."

"Woman like you has a lot of good years left in her. You should keep your eyes open," Frank said.

Irene was relieved when Frank left. She found another piece of mail for him, looked like it could be a letter from his granddaughter, but she didn't call after him to come back. He could get it tomorrow.

She read a postcard from Myrtle's granddaughter. Looked like she might be coming for a visit. And a card from Lillian's daughter, a college exchange student in Switzerland. She was hiking in the Alps. Irene didn't feel bad about reading post cards. People didn't put secrets in postcards. There was a long envelope for Lillian from her ex-husband, and Irene held it up to the window. Seemed like it was a check. For the life of her, Irene couldn't see the amount.

She put Etta's *Workbasket* and James Wilcox's *Presbyterian Life* in their boxes. She flipped through Lillian's *Vogue*. Why she got that, Irene never could figure. Not one of those outfits anyone in town would wear, not even Lillian.

■ ■ ■

Irene had always been a church person, Herbert too. She and Herbert went to church together most Sundays. Now the idea of finding comfort going to church didn't feel right. She wasn't sure what she believed. She couldn't bring herself to think about Herbert being off somewhere, either in heaven looking down on her or in hell being punished for what he did. Some people thought there was no question that's where he'd be because of how he died.

Must have seemed odd to people when she stopped going to church after once going almost every Sunday, but no one asked her why she didn't go anymore. It was simple. On the day of Herbert's funeral she was feeling about as sad and shocked and embarrassed as a person could be. She went to the restroom in the church basement before the service to check her hair and try to work up her courage to walk with John up to the front row past all those people and sit next to Herbert's mother and the rest of his family. She was in the rest room, the door locked, when she heard people talking outside. She knew Phyllis's voice, and the other one sounded like Mary.

"Things like this don't happen here. You knew Herbert as well as any of us. What do you think caused it?"

"I don't know any more than anyone else," Phyllis said, "but there must have been things that drove him to it. I don't think Irene was always an easy person to live with."

Irene heard them go up the stairs and waited a few minutes to open the door. Phyllis was the closest friend she had, like a sister, and to say a thing like that on the day of Herbert's funeral. It hurt almost as much as what Herbert had done.

Phyllis organized the whole funeral meal, stood behind the table and spread out the food everyone brought—ham and scalloped potatoes, cole slaw, applesauce, Jello and macaroni salads. She acted as neighborly as can be, and Irene thanked

She flipped through Lillian's* Vogue. *Why she got that, Irene could never figure. Not one of those outfits anyone in town would wear, not even Lillian.

her for taking care of it all. But, after Irene heard Phyllis say what she said, she wondered if Phyllis was doing it all for show, not because she cared.

Phyllis never asked Irene why things were different between them after Herbert died. She called a few times to invite Irene over for a meal or to go shopping, but didn't seem to give it a second thought when Irene said no.

If it weren't for Irene calling to ask Phyllis and Luther's boys to mow her grass or seeing one of them when they picked up the mail, she'd have had no contact at all. The empty lot between their houses might as well have been fifty miles wide.

Maybe Phyllis hadn't meant anything with what she said. People said things, just for the sake of talking, but why would she say something that hurtful? Had Herbert talked to Luther about Irene not being easy to live with? They'd all joked about her always wanting to keep the house clean, keeping after Herbert to pick up his socks. Is that all Phyllis meant?

When Irene was looking for her chocolate chip cookie recipe, she came across recipes Phyllis had given her when they baked Christmas cookies together. That was a time. Once Phyllis found a bottle of sherry in her cupboard and they drank a couple glasses, and then everything struck them funny. Lots of cookies got burned on the bottom that day. It's a wonder all of them weren't ruined. It had been a long time since Irene laughed like that, the way she and Phyllis used to laugh.

■ ■ ■

That afternoon Irene bagged up the mail, pulled down the blinds and locked the door. The sun was about to drop behind the mountains. The winter trees, starting to bud, glowed a hazy green. In a couple weeks trees would be covered with leaves and blossoms. How could spring come so quickly?

On the side of the road were a couple candy wrappers, Almond Joy and Hershey bar. Probably from Phyllis and Luther's boys walking home from the store after school. Irene stooped to pick them up and put them in her pocket. Those boys knew better than that.

Luther, or maybe the boys, had already pruned the raspberries, still looking like dried brambles, and they'd raked the winter mulch off the strawberries. All the berries, even the little blueberry bushes, had already grown. Everything had spread, and, all along, she still thought of the space between their houses as an empty lot.

She walked up the front walk to her house. Sweetness was asleep on the back of the sofa inside the picture window, a window so clean that Sweetness might have felt like she was outdoors. When Irene put the key in the lock, she heard a thump as Sweetness jumped down and ran to the door.

Irene bent down to stroke her, opened a can of cat food and put it in the bowl on the table.

"You'll have to eat alone, because I have things to do. Spring is coming, and we need to get fresh air in here."

The spring before, Irene hadn't taken the plastic off the inside of the windows. It was the last thing on her mind after Herbert did what he did. By the time it occurred to her it was time to take off the plastic and open the storm windows, it was already fall and getting cooler. She didn't bother.

She started with the plastic on the kitchen windows facing Luther and Phyllis's house, peeling off the tape Herbert had used to seal it around the window frames. It was holding tight. She was working on the second window, the plastic hanging halfway down, when she saw Phyllis's car pull in the driveway beyond the berry patch. Phyllis reached in the back seat for her groceries, grabbed the bags and knocked the car door shut with her hip. She stopped and looked toward Irene's house beyond the berry patch. Without thinking, Irene lifted her hand to wave. ■

HE SEEMS DIFFERENT, 1999, FROM THE SERIES *SOUL ERASED*, JOYCE SCOTT

High left corner zinnia sun

black and white above

the tilt and grin skeleton in

an x-ray purple shirtdress—:   Baby boy stands
already knee deep in the hill
both feet in the grave,   a sack
of bones with sweet straight teeth,
the pained grin of the mischievous
child. Curious tilt. Chubby cheeks &
forehead shine. Strange grey eyes.
The child who bites in the classroom.
Wants love but wants to sink his
no longer babyteeth into the subject.
He is the subject. He seems different.

Subject verb. Seeming looks like
enumerated bones. In future will he
be kept in a drawer? In future he
will be stored. ③ near the clavicle.
⑤ over the heart. The mountain holds
his feet. Little feet held in granite. Little
pelvis—: Little fish, what's leftover
after dinner? Someone has eaten
the eye. Picked clean meal
of scrunch-nosed kora smile—:
discarded. Not cement shoes, but
still—

LYRAE VAN CLIEF-STEFANON

SCORNED, HE IMPLODES, 1999, FROM THE SERIES *SOUL ERASED*, JOYCE SCOTT

A jutting full of eyes—: an outcropped
eye-cropping—: a seeing flame,
a mad-seeing tentacle, an unsightly
excess of seeing—: an assemblage of
eyeballs: eye-quilt—: two eye masses
opening out like a river's tributary. See
how he grew a shadow under
their gaze over his bones. See how
he has grown—: unwieldy, a woman's
hips over a small boy. His face now
a silver mask. ⑰ kneecap ⑳ anklebone
⑯ leg's long bone. One gun as long
as his leg. What's the thing at the
gun range you discharge your gun
into? Imagine it sees. ㉒ the big

toe. ⑤ over the heart. Label the
skeleton for the museum. In the
deep of the bullet receptacle some
one has placed a small black child.
He leans, awash in red, against the
hellgate that looks banally like a white
farm gate. The shadow child is failed

enfleshment, chalkboard black to score-
keep the bones. He undoes the safety and
ushers the oversized gun towards the other
boy's head; the other, holstered to his hips or
slung through pelvis bones. Patterned
throw—: a collection of dragon's eyes.
All this takes place at the dragon hour :—
his face, a sterling sparkle, an MRI,
a negative

GUNS AS ANGEL'S WINGS, 1999, FROM THE SERIES *SOUL ERASED*, JOYCE SCOTT

Starry night as texture, a wisp above the grave
Of the pink boned dead child. Pink as

Implantation blood.
Faint. A small tan coffin,

Its corners like a black girl's nails two years back.

The wisps might form themselves into an
Eye above his head, but don't—
Lush glyph of smoke. Coffin stood up on the hill
Like a stolen stele. Little Rose Li

In the coffin's womb—:

Guns make useless wings.
A shadow asleep in the hill in a contorted child's
Pose. Made of the hill. Placental. Impression

& ash. Remember

Mortal that thou art dust. Remember you are mortal.
An umbrella's point may emerge from the ground
Soon with erosion. A hand mirror.
Some other
Artifact.
Coffin double duties as headstone.
Rose Li, cherub, sturdy bones, stands inside as though for duel. Cowboys &
Emptiness—: childhood. Guns with no grip. Stone. This improbable not float.

LYRAE VAN CLIEF-STEFANON

REPENT, 1999, FROM THE SERIES *SOUL ERASED*, JOYCE SCOTT

The angel made of brush dance sinew

dances color up through strokes of muscle:

orange from arches up through knees

to mid thigh, red from hips to heart

out the shoulders spilling over into

wings, a faceless pink brown flutter

of head. Silvermask, left-handed, raises

his shooting arm sheepishly to show

where two extra arms have sprouted

from his shoulder. His chalkboard shadow

has expanded to hold his extra limbs, his

pelvis a spider that has grown two extra legs.

The bat sign points this side up. Meanwhile,

inside, an extra arm cuts through his spine.

Creature, creature, for conversation in dance

he dances atop an amorphous white world.

LYRAE VAN CLIEF-STEFANON

SAP

I ask the tree to register
Me and it stings—
What for...?
Some ridiculous itch
Nibbles, hails hate
Hiding plain, insight
A twitching
Claw-gripped pendant
Fixed against its
Bark lapels.
A glimpse and this

Network exposed,
An almost
Ancient urge to lick or for
A loam and petrichor
Scent, s'il vout plait,
Perfumier. Something to match

the umbered amber drip, its
grip, its scratch, its un-
Straight stretch
Towards warning.
Femme, Look up!
That patch of flame
In the limb pit—worry
Winter amplifies. Will it
Spread? Will spring
Wrest mourning with
Its feckless inflammation
Of flowers. Will me to pick

Some new arboreal
Altar to shove adoration
Toward? Effulgent
Ignorance, but real—such
Anxiety!—this. I would miss
It if it changed
Too much. My favorite,
I call it friend.

LYRAE VAN CLIEF-STEFANON

“TO BELIEVE IN THIS LIVING—”

All time is wasted.
I withered mine to space, nights
imperfecting formulas. Elegance
as :—: as
being both the church
and funk of always :—:
always a rumpled coverlet
we can’t imagine
sharing, having
shared.
          I can’t turn to
the way flowers wilt, immediate
impulse, toward peonies’ pink lilt,
their lying down, droop, a silkening. And then
the urge to slink in
a pink slip. An elegance
in letting myself
go—
whither?—in that degree, to that

extent—as
the churchy hmmm of background singers
all humming their assent.

LYRAE VAN CLIEF-STEFANON

SOME THOUGHTS ON MARRIAGE BEFORE I WED

REBECCA GAYLE HOWELL

By one notion, Cleo rose in the Van Lear morning. He'd dress, shout something smart to Frankie as her goodbye, drive to Druther's in Paintsville and drink his coffee with the boys, then leave it all behind for that day's make-or-break at Bob's Pay Lake. Cleo'd park a straight line into that gravel lot, then raise the hatch on his Chevette to take out the six gleaming shark poles he knew could work the only job he had, to hook Old 69, the resident mud cat, a fish as large as a lie no one believed. All the men put their dollars in that cat's jar, a good-sport Powerball for the one of them who would pull him up out of his loungey, bottom-feeding privacies, his forgotten holler I'm sure 69 preferred to be forgotten in.

■ ■ ■

I never knew Cleo. He was my love's daddy's daddy, a man who I've been told was gentle and kind, with enough violence in him to make Frankie laugh off her old life. Together, they were hoarders; between the wiles of *Time* magazines and electronic parts, paths cut through their home, making way to the necessaries. In Cleo's day Van Lear was a Consolidated town. He'd mined, briefly, as a scab, but his career was cards and liquor. He told his family he was a rich man, kept wads of money in his pocket, rolls of money, to show. The house sat on Silk Stocking Loop and presented itself like a boss's house, with a porch that rose to a second-story roof by way of four grand, vinyl-sided columns. Triumphant and drunk, Cleo would clean out the dress store for Frankie just to see her smile. Then he'd lose it all the next night; return her dresses in the day's light. Big was Cleo's style; I can see those shark poles dug into the beach's curve, a neat, strategic row, the sure future. "Mix up some biscuits and gravy, Frankie! I'm taking this boy fishing!" he'd say to the whole house, the whole town, if it would only listen.

■ ■ ■

The son of Cleo had a different style: bigger. Bigger shouting. Bigger praying. Harder hitting. A miner, exhausted from working his double shift, he fell asleep driving home one early morning, sent his truck end over end over end in an empty field. Paralyzed on one side of his body and for ten years more he terrorized his family. When his wife finally reached her courage, she left him, then he married another woman, and another.

■ ■ ■

My people prefer to be small. Grandaddy raised his family on Buckhorn, about a hundred miles from Cleo and Frankie, on an isolated few acres where he and my grandma toiled to feed their ten kids and the annual pig. He'd drank rotgut when he was young, but did not run it, as his brothers did. Instead he sobered into a silence and rolled his own. "All your grandfather wanted was to be up in that holler with his family, where everybody else would leave him alone," my mother's repeated warning against—what? —not seeing the world, I suppose, which I have done, thanks entirely to my mother's leave-taking of that family when she was a girl.

■ ■ ■

She likes to fish, my mom. After she reached her courage and left my father, a boyfriend came around who sold fast cars and who showed up many a night at our door in a Corvette or a Firebird, soused and bullying; my mother shouting at me to call the police. On the good Saturdays, Kenneth would take her fishing, and sometimes we'd all congregate to fry what they'd caught, eat together, play cards together, until the sun fell. He was the only boyfriend, the risk my mom took. After she left him, for years after, we'd be at the doctor's office or the mall only to find upon our return another dead fish tied to the car's door handle. I often think about Frankie. She had "the sight," I'm told, ESP. She could see into the veil and tell what would soon happen, but she could not see her son for who he was, or her husband; or, she did and did not mind.

■ ■ ■

A pay lake is a dirty place. Shallow, stagnant waters teeming with old-growth fish meant for the wild rivers. Trophies, they call the flatheads and blues, most of them twenty years-old and big as me. As in, something you win. As in, yours. A catfish has no scales on her skin. She's fleshy and with those long whiskers; all of it, her whole body, a sensor that can smell and taste and hear by touch, by nearness. She'll spend her day in quiescence, under some rock, still, but alert; we'll say she's sleeping but we're wrong.

■ ■ ■

Before Pangea, all of Kentucky was algae; a promise secured under the sea. Today, we are landlocked. We fake our lakes and bury our headstreams. We import drinking water from Virginia. We don't know each other or each other's places or our own. The first time I ever was in Van Lear my love took me there. It was early days for our affair, snow still on the ground. We drove through rows of houses sheltering dealers and users, neighbors with cue balls for eyes, as well as the rows of tidy homes belonging to the Church of Christ faithful, the neighbors with a plan. Since 1945, since the war was won, Van Lear has been unincorporated; officially, it is an accident of buildings, an undetermined human population with no representation and no boundaries; a place that exists because of tradition. Because that's the way it's always been. Because we all got to have someone. As my love drove that cold day I watched out the window, wondering to God how any of us choose each other, if not by tradition. But that's another story worth believing only if you have a dollar in the jar. ■

THE GRANNY WOMAN'S NOTE

When serving birth
Summon the womb
Open every window
every door to the house

to the barn to the room
Let them come on through
those cold rains, rot-lonely flies
all the waspers of this world

Tell them now is the time

And when your job is other
when they've declared
a body a corpse
Stay up all night

no matter

the hour or ghost
When serving death
again serve birth
Open

every window
every door Draw close
to that chest once filled
with God's air

And place your mortal ear
there, listen
for what this womb will
invite in you

REBECCA GAYLE HOWELL

THE BASKETMAKER'S NOTE

They're called staves, right?

Stave: as in, to break a thing by turning it inward
as in, to stay, as in, don't be afraid, my darling girl,

be the strong one, hidden
and planted, the underpinning

around which all the rest gets wound

REBECCA GAYLE HOWELL

THE STONE CARVER'S NOTE

To whatever home you call home—
a door, locked; a mother's place;
a family, that dream state—compare
When you find the big stone rock,
the one bigger than all that,
put your skull face to her skull face,
stand Still Let, what?—God, Time,
Boredom—shade your eyes
Then, with night-sight watch
how song fills air with old unrest,
disturbs snake and creek,
moves, erodes Even this strong rock,
both gate and guard, smooths
Even you Forget trinkets
Here, the map we grave To begin,
leave home Go home
Enter the wood's inscape

REBECCA GAYLE HOWELL

BARELY RUNNABLE

JAKE MAYNARD

One week after record rainfall burst the riverbanks of southern West Virginia, destroying homes and roads and ending twenty-six lives, I gawked at the destruction I passed on the two-lane highway. Downed trees, culverts washed away, sheds knocked cockeyed. Hundreds were still displaced, many more still without electricity. It was mid-summer. Hot, cloudless, and bright. I was headed to Fayette County, near the heart of the damage, to spend the weekend at an "adventure resort." There, I would be paid 400 dollars to write a short narrative promoting their main attraction—whitewater rafting on the Gauley River.

I wasn't to be rafting, though. The Gauley was too flooded to raft. But there were deadlines to make, promos to release. Therefore, as the marketing company explained to me, "the story will require research and some imagination."

What they meant was that they wanted a fake narrative they would publish as travelogue, as truth. They wanted "vivid and colorful" language. Something *picturesque, majestic, fulfilling, resplendent*, etc. They'd hired me, in part, because my CV showed I was "also a fiction writer." But name a writer who doesn't tell a little fiction.

Big blue resort signs pointed me—like I would be otherwise incredulous—down a county road with ditches still choking on flotsam. The road wound through a little town where all the once-identical company houses had turned different shades of haggard, like the place where I grew up. Past town, the resort's entrance appeared: a billboard, fresh blacktop, and a pond the color of a peacock.

At the log-faced Welcome Center, the tattooed hostess surprised me with the news that I'd be rafting The Gauley after all. And instead of the usual summer current, we'd be rafting at 9,000 cubic feet per second—the highest flow that they would take guests on, per industry policy. "You'll be on the first trip since the flood!" she told me. "There's no real way of telling what you're gonna find out there."

Across a parking lot, I found the resort's bar & grill, a structural twin to the Welcome Center. It was called The Lost Paddle, and inside it looked like Applebee's had tried to launch a chain of dive bars. At a barstool, two free beers later, I googled Gauley River. Google read my mind, suggesting "Gauley River Deaths." I stopped myself from reading the statistics. Instead I found a site that provided up-to-the-minute gauges of the river's height. In bold red letters, it said the river was "Not Runnable." Good, I thought. Maybe this was official. Maybe I could just drive home and imagine the whole piece.

The Lost Paddle was running a special: one dollar from the sale of every West Virginia-made beer would be donated to flood relief efforts. Drinking my charity beer, I listened to two dreadlocked bartenders discussing the flood. One person—*one body*—was still missing. They seemed shaken-up and rightly so. This was their community. But they still had to sell T-shirts and rent cabins and take people down the river, riding the same water that'd done the deed.

I checked the site again. In electric green it read, "Barely Runnable."

■ ■ ■

The backside of the bar opened to a veranda overlooking the "Wonderland Waterpark"—a two-acre lake crowded with zip lines and giant inflatable pool toys. Some were shaped like ships, others like castles. Kids and shameless adults climbed the toys and jumped headlong into the water. The resort staff milled around the lake after their shifts, smoking and discussing work. I found a circle of grimy raft guides and told them I was a travel writer, not mentioning that my five stars had been pre-paid. I asked about the flood. With kayaks and rafts in tow, they said, they'd driven the swamped valleys, searching for trapped people and animals.

One guide, the only one dressed like a soccer dad, told me about an old woman who'd died. Howard's Creek, one county over, had burst its banks and flooded her creekside home. She'd climbed to the upstairs, then the attic, and then the roof. The house floated away with her on it, catching fire when the gas line sheared. She clung to a tree, badly burned, through the night. There's a video online of her burning house, floating down the creek like a boat in a Norse funeral.

"We could hear her," he told me. "We could even talk to her. We could have gotten to her with a kayak. Even if I had to just cling to the tree with her all night, I would have."

He said the local fire department, which was managing the rescue effort, wouldn't let him help because of something to do with insurance. "If your house is on fire, you call a fireman," he said. "If you're trapped in a flood you should call a raft guide."

■ ■ ■

Geologically speaking, The Gauley is one of the oldest rivers in North America. But in another sense it's a modern construction. Beginning as a bog on one of West Virginia's highest mountains, The Gauley runs southwest for about a hundred miles through steep mountains that stop Midwestern clouds and shake the rain out of them. The Gauley used to cause severe flooding way downriver in Charleston, West Virginia's capital. In 1960 the Army Corps of Engineers decided to dam it. The process took six years, displaced the community of Gad, and created a four square-mile lake. A cemetery was flooded in the process, the bodies relocated only if the next of kin requested it.

Each fall, the Corps drains the dam and, for a few weekends a year, The Gauley becomes one of the best whitewater rivers in the country. In the summer it's supposed to be shallow and pittering. But the extreme rainfall had lifted the water level of the lake by thirty-eight feet. Worried for the dam's integrity, they'd been forced to open the dam wide for a few hours, releasing water at twenty times the usual flow. That much pressure could alter the river, the rapids. "It could be a whole new river," the tattooed hostess had told me. I knew I shouldn't write as much; my experience should be replicable by any potential visitors.

■ ■ ■

The next morning I signed waivers releasing liability for everything from drowning to theft to snake bites to "slippery mud." Then, thirty hokey tourists and I loaded onto an old school bus with a trailer of stacked rafts hitched to the back. To make more room, the guides made us wear our bright yellow life-vests and helmets during the bus ride. All of the tourists were white, sunscreen white. Some couples, families, aging buddies trying to reconnect. Then there was the

The alders and laurel that grew along the banks were all bent downriver, slicked back like a greaser's haircut.

Christian young men's group from Iowa that had just finished a few days of "flood relief aid." Their leader—a little goateed guy with barbed wire tattooed around his bicep—kept telling his guys to "go big or go home." He said it again and again, slapping each teen on the back of his helmet.

"Are you ready to party on the Gauley?" a guide hollered from the front of bus, pumping a fist into the air.

"Yes."

"You can do better!" he hollered.

"Yes!"

When the guides told us of the river's dangers, I hoped they were exaggerating. I'd once known a raft guide who liked to terrify his clients with fake stories of deadly undercurrents on the safe river where he worked. He reasoned that by making the guests more afraid, they'd tip him better when they survived. His job, like mine, was in selling untruth.

Our guide explained that The Gauley's hydraulic currents can bore holes straight through the center of submerged boulders. Occasionally these holes are the size of a car. Occasionally these holes are just big enough to inhale a person, but not big enough to spit them out the other side. Rafters call these "retirement holes." When, rarely, someone is lost in a retirement hole, the Army Corps has to turn off the river to retrieve the body. Slowly, the water level drops as other rafters ride out the last of the water ejected from the dam. Sometimes the reduced pressure lets the body pop out and rise to the surface. Other times the river just drops until they meet.

■ ■ ■

The Gauley was brown and foaming, half again as wide as I'd seen in the pictures. The alders and laurel that grew along the banks were all bent downriver, slicked back like a greaser's haircut. Matted leaves were stuck in the trees, fifteen feet above the river, the high water mark from the dam release.

The other tourists tried to make themselves useful by tightening each other's life jackets. Two strong guys in their late twenties caught my attention. They wore expensive, water-wicking clothes and swaggered along the river's edge. They were my mark. The marketing company had told me who to write for: "A guy in is mid-twenties/early thirties who has a good job or is seeking higher education. Is an extreme, thrill-seeker who enjoys adrenaline activities and wants to break up the monotony of adulthood. Doesn't hesitate to spend money to have a good time. Also attends concerts, initiates group outdoor trips, and paddles hard and parties harder."

One of the guys, I learned by eavesdropping, was in medical school. The other did something with clients and accounts. And what luck—these shmucks were to be in my boat. They were paying $265.00 each for this.

I met the rest of my crew. The shmucks had each brought a quiet girlfriend, eyes heavy with mascara. Our guide was a big redhead named Derek and along with him was a guide-in-training. She was dressed in a shiny black neoprene wetsuit stretched tight against her large middle. She wore a white lifejacket and a black helmet with huge white stickers on the sides. The stickers looked like the eyespots some animals develop for protection. When she put the helmet on, she looked strikingly like an orca.

Together we carried the raft to the river's edge and hopped in. Derek walked us through the commands for paddling and told us we could call him by one of many names: Derek, D-rick, D-Rock, D-Bag or just D. I chose D-rick because the shmucks went with D-Rock.

And then it was time to party on the Gauley.

■ ■ ■

Psychologists say that most fears are learned through experience, family, culture, etc. There are a few, though, that are lodged deep in our genetic coding. Think: darkness, snakes, spiders, murky water. Brain scan technology illuminates this. When shown videos of brown, frothing rapids, something in your primitive brain lights up. I thought about this as we went through the first few rapids; I was supposed to be afraid. Choosing to be afraid was the point. But on our raft, one of the girlfriends seemed unable to quiet her raging medulla oblongata. Every time we hit whitewater she faked a loss of balance and threw herself to the center of the boat, away from the slippery edges where you sit to paddle. She thought she would be safer in the middle. And she was probably right. That is, until our raft went ass-over-tincups in the biggest rapid on the middle Gauley.

We were the second of the four boats to go through. The first had skirted the rapid to the right, missing the giant haystack of a wave that recirculated in the center of the river. We hit it dead center. The nose of the boat reared up like a wheelie gone awry. I saw foamy white, pale blue sky. An empty space where the schmucks were supposed to be.

I was in the boat, then the water. It was that immediate. Boat / water—the cold angry shock of it. I don't remember swimming. Or rising to the surface. Just waves and the upside-down raft next to me. I grabbed ahold and scanned the horizon for my crew. Nothing but river. The river was everything, everything and every direction.

When the boat reached a piece of steady water the world reappeared. I saw the guide-in-training holding onto the back of the raft, gagging water. D-Rick swam up from behind, climbed onto the flipped raft, attached a strap, and threw himself backward in the water, righting it. I kicked and pulled and scrambled back into the boat. The guide-in-training could not make it back in, so I pulled her back in like I'd been instructed beforehand. We fell backward into the raft and her face landed exactly in my crotch. Another raft had picked up the schmucks and their quiet girlfriends as they floated downriver. The fearful girlfriend had been knocked under by a recirculating current and she looked green in the face. The schmucks hooted and hollered about how much fun they'd had. We picked them up from the other raft and collected our paddles from the slack water. I was shivering. Guide-in-training was still coughing up river. D-Rick said, "Well, that rapid's not the same as it used to be." The other guides were already heckling him.

We stopped at a sandbar for lunch and ate food fit for a Methodist potluck. Once dry, I began to feel the pull of the schmucks' enthusiasm. Fun—it *had* been fun. It felt authentic, or something like it. I knew the river was dammed, not wild, but for a minute I didn't care. The Army Corps had shaped the river, and I would shape a bullshit travelogue about it. So what. Justifications are everywhere if you look for them.

After lunch we paddled toward the last three rapids and the take-out, where, we were told, a cooler of beer waited. D-rick said that we were lucky because the church group didn't drink. There'd be more beer for us. The shmucks were grinning and a human color had returned to the scared girlfriend. The travelogue was already taking shape in my head. Something-something about a gathering of old college buddies, like the schmucks, who met each year to chase adrenaline. One of them could be a coward who finds his courage after taking a swim in the mighty Gauley River. His friends would pull him back into the boat, strengthening their bond and staving off the doldrums of adulthood. Ta-da.

But as we ran the rapids, I became my own story. The shmucks and girlfriends and I clanked our paddles in celebration. At one point I hooted *woo-hooo,* calling to the fake thing now becoming real.

We came to the last rapid and D-Rick warned us of an undercut rock on river-right. If you hit the water, he said, "Swim as hard as you possibly can towards river-left and don't stop until you hit the shore." We took the safe route and skirted the rapid to the left. The next boat canted sideways and nearly flipped. Two of the church group toppled in, one from each side of the boat. A heavy kid landed in the still water at river left. A muscular kid was sucked into the rapid. His helmet disappeared, reappeared, and went under again.

The guides blew their orange whistles. We scanned the water from the eddy downriver. Painful seconds passed. He popped up and was walloped through the waves. Towards river left, the heavy kid bobbed in the slack water like an apple. They told him to swim to shore and made for the muscular kid, who flailed ten yards downriver. When they got to him, he was screaming.

Their raft beached in a whirl of commotion. The muscular kid lay skyfaced on the floor of the boat, guides and church kids circling him. The medical-student schmuck jumped from

The guides blew their orange whistles. We scanned the water from the eddy downriver. Painful seconds passed.

our boat and thrashed through the knee-deep water toward him. D-rick told us to give them some room.

After a few minutes they lifted the kid up and walked him to the beach. His left arm was dislocated at the shoulder, deforming the silhouette of him against the sun. He wailed and babbled. Close by, the church group kneeled and prayed like a football team encircling an injured quarterback. I found the cooler and grabbed two beers. I opened one and placed the other in my upturned helmet that I'd nested in the crook of my arm, like a baby. The medical student—who I'd decided was not a schmuck—was taking charge of the kid's care, asking him calm questions about the scale of his pain. But the kid wouldn't answer questions. Instead, he talked about the undercut rock. He said he'd been pulled under it; he'd felt the rock on top him. And why had the hole spit him out? It was Jesus, Jesus had spared him. His face was streaked with tears.

Later, D-Rick told me what actually happened. The kid was likely thrust down to the river bottom by an undercurrent. When he rose, arms lifted, he bashed into the underside of the raft, popping his shoulder. He'd been nowhere near the retirement hole. They spent thirty minutes trying to convince the kid to let them set the dislocated shoulder. The church buddies whispered among themselves and thanked god. It was all incredibly awkward. By the riverbank, I heard one of the church kids say, "He needs to stop being such a pussy and get on with this." Eventually they did set the socket, and we all heard the scream.

Because of the flooding, the dirt road from the river was a pitted mess that took forty minutes to climb. Some homes along the road were still without their power lines. One was missing its bridge. We hit a pothole and the kid's shoulder dropped from its socket. They set it. It happened again. Each time we sat in silence, slurping beers over the thrumming engine. The kid sobbed as the medical student adjusted his makeshift sling.

When we finally hit blacktop, we all started chatting.

■ ■ ■

The travelogue took me ninety minutes to write. I did it as soon as I got home, and a few days later I made small revisions when the company said it should be "more positive."

It would take a week before I began to churn with the hypocrisy, the questioning. After my check was deposited and my sunburn had molted, I would sit with the moths on my porch and work to extract some selfish meaning. Something

something about how safe we've become. About the flooded cemetery, about poverty and geography. I don't know—something about rafting the killing water to feel alive.

But even now, despite the ironies, I can't shake the way I'd felt when that bus hit blacktop. On the bus, I didn't care about the flood or my dishonest writing. On the bus, I was dirt-flecked and half-drunk. I was tired and stupid. And I wanted to laugh and drink and bullshit with all the other tired and stupid people. I wasn't worried about authenticity, or complicity, or any of the other *-icities* that keep me up too late. Because I felt safe, and real, and happy. Happier than I'd felt in a long time. ■

ABSCISSION

September arced across the mountains, a warm
hay-breeze swirled among the graven stones, nudged
faded oak leaves to chatter, stirred the scent of carnations
and the sharp odor of mums that rose from that patch of
turned earth.

The day a mountain postcard, dogwoods rusted at woods'
edge
behind the church and buckeyes blazed among the green.
For weeks, that perfect sky taunted me and turned
into October—those days that cause me to chant Yeats
as I walk the dry paths and shuffle gold with my feet.

November came to save me. The rain dripped from eaves,
felled the gaudy leaves, and closed the sky
so I could shut the windows, light the fire, and keen into
my tea.

JANE HICKS

TAKE THIS LEAF

...read these leaves in the open air every season, every year of your life. —Walt Whitman

Open to air and sky, one feels none other
than small, a particle, a part, a leaf, a blade of
a great whole. Feel the rustle, stir, and hum as all
moves together, give and get cycles of earth, air, sun, and
    water.
The bob of flower heads as bees lift away,
whir of hummingbird wing, feather that floats to earth.
All binds. The moth wing sets
waves in motion, a mountain's face peels away,
slides to its feet. A sigh upon leaves,
a gift returned, sweat on a brow, rain anew.
The sun, a lamp, a hearth, what needs be
when needs be. Small. All crouch small
beneath the vault of the sky, or held in the bowl
of the mountains, washed in light,
flow out free where science and soul meet.

JANE HICKS

FOLLOW

I waved my hand over the patch, but made no shadow
in the place. —Maurice Manning

The chemo clouds and veils thought,
a stream hits a rock dam, splashes, diffused,
lost but to weeds and mud. A reader cannot read,
follow the course of thought through a chapter,
the flow of an essay, the journey of an article.
The poem saves, its brevity runs thought
to a stop, grasped, apprehended.
Reread, underline, pause, image clear,
word-echo provokes, the thought hovers, takes
form. Step by step, poems like creek
stones or tree-blazed marks bring one through
forest, tangled and bare, to tangled
and green after a lost winter,
underlined words a pocket of found
treasure, proof of the trail and the guide.

JANE HICKS

PERSIST

Sun-dappled drowsy fawns sprang
up at every turn of the trail last spring.
The doe deposited them, always apart,
in thickets, brush piles, honeysuckle warrens,
collected them at day's end. I often saw them
in shadows, suckled in the gloaming,
my walks timed to disturb them least until they grew
nimble, spooked less, learned to lay low.

Sleek-muscled, wary, the wood sprites, mother and
daughters
still appear as three, still graze in woods-edge dawns
and open field twilights. Fall brought forth the mother
wounded,
shot across the shoulder, flesh ripped raw, fur pulled away,
spine spared. I watched, hoped she would not succumb
—she persisted.
Spring, timid this year, finds her healed, graceful, still
mother to beauty.

I ponder the doe, her healing given as a sign,
I persist. Chemicals course through, fog my words,
tear my hair from me, leave a specter's reflection.
The fall wounded us all on the ridge, my breast, stitched,
cancer excised, healed as the doe healed.

JANE HICKS

AN *APPALACHIAN HERITAGE* CONVERSATION WITH

LYRAE VAN CLIEF-STEFANON & REBECCA GAYLE HOWELL

When the 2017 Appalachian Symposium was held at Berea College last fall, expectations were high. After all, the debut of the biennial event in September 2015 had set a high bar, when thirty of Appalachia's most celebrated and active writers had gathered to discuss the current state of literature and Appalachian culture. Instead of another large assemblage, founder Silas House had decided that subsequent events would focus on one or two writers, who would share their work and expertise over the course of two days.

The second symposium did not disappoint, featuring two of the region's—and the country's—finest poets: Lyrae Van Clief-Stefanon, a National Book Award finalist for her 2009 collection *Open Interval* and a Cave Canaam Award winner, and Rebecca Gayle Howell, author of the acclaimed collections *American Purgatory* and *Render / An Apocalypse*, and poetry editor of *Oxford American*.

In between giving readings and teaching workshops, Van Clief-Stefanon and Howell engaged in a riveting, candid public conversation with House that examined Appalachian, African-American and working class identity; American politics; and the role of the artist in contemporary America. This conversation has been edited for length.

■ ■ ■

SILAS HOUSE: One reason we have the Appalachian Symposium is because we want Appalachia to be thought of not only as a local place but as a global place. One of the great pieces of Appalachian Literature is "The Brier Sermon" by Jim Wayne Miller. In it, he says, "We don't have to think ridge to ridge anymore. We can think ocean to ocean." I'm wondering how you all respond to that idea of Appalachia as simultaneously very local and very global.

LYRAE VAN CLIEF-STEFANON: I was thinking this morning—it hadn't occurred to me ever to sit and figure out how long I've lived in Appalachia until I knew that you were going to ask us questions about it, and I realized that I've lived in Appalachia for half my life, and that was shocking to me. I think that it is so tied up for me in family. Not just in terms of family drawing you in, but also family that you flinch from, because family for me has as much flinch as drawing-in in it. That's where my mind goes with that question of the ways in which families are born, made, and found, and the way that those connections can be global of those born, made, and found families. You're always finding those connections... What are the different ways in which we are tied to each other across the planet, and how can we move through them and make them visible so [that becomes] a thing we keep in our minds more often?

How do we keep [that] in our minds, instead of having our minds constantly [be] disciplined into shaping and thinking in ways that I feel like are not good for us as human beings [or] not good for us as people in this country? [It's] not good for us as human beings to constantly be disciplined into thinking, *This is how we have to think and talk about this, and this is the way that we know these identities.* For myself, [I try] not to think about it in terms of claim but in terms of an expansion.

REBECCA GAYLE HOWELL: I have been processing my sense of place through an idea of Wendell Berry's use of the word economy and his lifting it up as a metaphor and a word that might mean new things in new contexts. Last night, *Thoughts in the Presence of Fear* [a documentary about Berry] came on KET [Kentucky Educational Television], and I was reminded that it's really just Wendell reading his essay "Thoughts on the Presence of Fear," which he wrote on the anniversary of September 11th. I was reminded, hearing him read it, that he's constantly saying, "We need a peaceable economy."

Lyrae Van Clief-Stefanon

My answer to this question is maybe the problem is not that we are not thinking ocean to ocean. Maybe the problem is we are born into a life and a livelihood that is inevitably ocean to ocean, and we are choosing to not be *aware* of it. So, we are thinking ocean to ocean in a global economic sense—we are pieces and parts of that globalized economy, and yet we are not aware of our global role in that. That denial and that silence allows for a lot of sickness. In some ways, I'm more interested in what happens if we do truly think ridge to ridge, meaning, what happens when we *do* know our neighbors? What happens when our food system *is* that local? What happens when our memory is localized, our love for each other? Maybe there is a liberty waiting in that.

SH: The older I get, the more I want my circle to be smaller and smaller. Do you find that, too? The more I learn about life and other people, the fewer people I want to know. It's sort of that same idea. While I want my circle to be smaller, I also want my knowledge to be broader. Since [Rebecca] mentioned Wendell Berry, I wonder, [Lyrae], if you wouldn't mind talking about what you were telling me about driving across the country with Wendell Berry['s work].

LVC-S: After the verdict came out in the Trayvon Martin case, I was so upset; I was just through. I was just through with America, just done. I already had issues with rage, with just being angry all the time, and I didn't feel like just being rageful. I thought, *what can I do in this moment to make myself feel better?* I grabbed a collection of Wendell Berry's poems and I got in my car, and I drove from Ithaca [New York] to Montana to Glacier National Park and back...I kept thinking about that piece [where] he writes about having scarred the land and feeling so sorry for it. But then, last night and this morning and this week, I was thinking about it like, *no, it's because of the way that Wendell Berry writes about the darkness.* He's one of the rare people who writes about the darkness in a way that makes sense to me and that doesn't fall into that rut—which I think is there in the language that people fall into—where the darkness is everything bad and terrible and [something] you want to get away from and you're terrified by. [He is] somebody who's actually being conscious with language in the same way that he is with the land—that kind of ties into that kind of thinking about identity you were just asking about.

There's this great line in one of Lucille Clifton's poems ["won't you celebrate with me"] where she says, *born in Babylon / both nonwhite and woman / what did I see to be except myself?* That sense of thinking about the region and my connection to it and how that connection works—I always refer to the South as an imaginary place where real things happen...Even though I'm not from Appalachia, I feel like it's a place where I belong. That sense of space in which you can be, in terms of the ways I think about being a black woman in this world, and how everything is just kind of *this is where you cannot be. You cannot be here, you cannot be here, you cannot be here.* So, to be in a space where I feel like *this is where I'm meant to be,* and my being able to be an author in that space—there's something sacred.

SH: People can have such a narrow view of what it means to be Appalachian. Some think you have to be born here. Some think you have to live here your whole life. I tend to think it's more about consciousness and how conscious you are of the place, and how you serve the place, and how you care about the place. Sometimes that caring about the place is questioning the place, loving it and hating it, everything in between and all that. I'll be honest—I had

Rebecca Gayle Howell

pushback from people that you two are not "Appalachian enough" to be part of The Appalachian Symposium. What I said most loudly was, "That's why we invited them. Because somebody like you would question their Appalachianness." They're basing that just on a standard bio without having any real knowledge of who you both are.

RGH: First of all, I just want to say that I think that critique sounds a little too much like *you're not black enough* or *you're not man enough* or *you're not American enough.* It's a really dangerous way to think.

Second, my mother was the daughter of subsistence farmers in Perry County [Kentucky]—the agrarian economy before the industrial economy in Appalachia had long gone. Her daddy had been raised in it. Her daddy refused to go to work [in the] coal [mines] or the railroads and instead decided to raise his family off the economy of the land. If they didn't grow it or make it or barter for it, usually a hog, they didn't have it. They did, however, have ten children, five boys, five girls.

[My mom] left her hollow at fifteen because her parents looked at her one day and said, "We can't afford the books for school anymore, so you can't go to school anymore." It didn't matter that she loved to learn and read so much so that she hurt her eyes reading in the dark after the rest of the family had gone to bed in their two-room house. She leaves... for a grown-up life [in] Louisville with [the promise of a job as a nanny for a family and that she could finish school. But the woman] locks my mom in her house and makes her an indentured servant. She ends up having to flee in the middle of the night. That's the context for the fact that my mom was a girl working a job and laying in bed at night, practicing losing her accent, practicing standard American English pronunciations over and over and over again, so that no one would know she was a hillbilly, so that she wouldn't lose her job, so that she wouldn't be made fun of.

So no—I don't have even the beginning of the understanding of the Appalachian dialect. No, I wasn't raised in the hills because my mother left and did everything she could to pass [as not Appalachian]. [But] I trace my bloodline there. Those are my people.

LVC-S: When I started thinking about what drove me from Florida [where I grew up] into Lexington, Rockbridge County, Virginia, it was two things. It was a change in the law that happened when I was in high school—the Hazelwood decision [where] the Supreme Court...said that student publications... didn't have First Amendment rights. I was the editor of my high school newspaper, and suddenly that decision comes down. And then...Tiananmen [Square] happened. There was a [dissident named] Wu'er Kaixi. He was one of the people who got an audience with Li Peng [then Premier of the People's Republic of China]...I'm seeing and hearing of this kid who's across the world. He's eighteen. He's on hunger strike, he's in his pajamas. And I'm thinking, *I'm going to go to school and be a journalist. I'm going to meet him to interview him, and we are going to fall in love and have revolutionary babies.* That's how my brain was working at eighteen.

Now, the route to that, to me—Florida girl that I was—was to go off to school. Washington and Lee [University] was the first journalism school in America, and so that's the school I picked. That's how I ended up in Virginia. And then [I found myself at Penn State] in graduate school [with Appalachian poet Lisa Parker]. We're the only two southerners. Everybody treats us like we're complete frigging idiots because we are Southern, and we're just like [to each other], *hey, you seem really familiar to me.* The more that we talk, the more familiar we are, and she takes me home to her house in Virginia for a singing. Her granddaddy, [with] generations of people in there singing, leans over to Lisa [and] says [about me], "That's good people." The rest of the family's like, "Well, you ain't never getting out of here now." So, suddenly, I have an Appalachian family. If you go to our mom's house, you can't tell her she didn't raise me. You cannot tell that I did not grow up right there. Faye Whitt, Grandma, would say to me, "Your heart knows where home is. This is my grandbaby."

So there's all these different threads that pull you into a space of being...There's no place in my life, there's no identity that I've inhabited, where I wasn't told, "You are not black enough." I was never girl enough, you know? I was queer, so I wasn't straight enough. I was not black enough. And so, yeah, I'm just more interested in all those threads and connections and the way they come together than in that argument [about not "being enough" of something].

SH: Since the [2016 presidential] election, the South and Appalachia keeps getting held up as the worst of [America], right? It seems like nobody else is at fault for that but Southerners and Appalachians. How do you respond when you see that happening?

RGH: I'm going to go back to the last question for a minute, but [what] comes to my mind is *who **isn't** Appalachian?* in the sense that what I was saying earlier. If we are the bellwether, if we are the ground zero of what happens in the corporatocracy—what the fallout is, what it looks like when it's done doing its business—then the rest of the country needs to be paying real close attention, because we're all part of this system. That's what I mean when I say we all ought to start looking ridge to ridge or hollow to hollow—real close.

To that end, then, I think that because we don't want to acknowledge our culpability in this system, globally, nationally—just like I think we don't want to acknowledge our culpability in the brutalities of American racism or the patriarchy—because we don't want to have to get people to come to Jesus about that, we have a natural disposition to start pointing fingers. *Well, racism is the South's fault; Trump is Appalachia's fault.*

I'll tell you this. There's a West Virginia photographer named Lisa Emaleh. The blame game [about the election had] really started to come down the pike. I was at my desk at the *Oxford American* when Lisa called me, and she said, "I just am so angry every time one of these stories hits the news." And she said, "I want to do something." And I said, "Well, let's do a little something."

So she and I got into the car and started traveling around Arkansas together and documenting. I was interviewing people, and she was photographing people, and trying to find people who had voted for Trump. Every single person we found and talked to was not only wealthy—they were a millionaire. These people went out of their way to express the amount of their wealth. These are not poor white people who put this man into office. These are white people with means who are scared shitless of losing those means.

LVC-S: Since the election—since *before* the election—I was the person who was running around in my town saying, "Hey,

hey, hey, the thing's coming!" And then people were saying to me, "How do you know?" And I said, "The sight runs in my family." That's not acceptable knowledge. And I'm saying, "No, he's going to win." And they're saying, "It's not possible what you're saying is going to happen. Numbers say that it's not possible." All of this stuff, blah, blah, blah.

And I'm saying, "Hey, the sight runs in my family, and so here's this thing that's gonna happen." And ever since then, since not being paid attention to and not listened to, I've been going back and delving through particular histories.

I'm obsessed right now with Phillis Wheatley—just obsessed. My poem "Migration" keeps saying "black is an ardor" and everything like that because Miss Phillis writes in her poem "On Imagination," *T'was an intrinsic ardor bid me write.* You know, everybody likes to tell [her] story like that that little girl was taught to read and all this other kind of fabulous stuff happened as a result of it. [But] I keep thinking about the fact that that seven-year-old got in those people's houses, and she picked up a piece of coal and she started writing on the wall, and that is the thing that precipitated teaching her to read. They say it like it's this happy story, and I'm like, *what was that baby writing on their wall?* I mean this. I'm really trying to figure out—when she picks up that coal and starts writing on the walls, what is she writing that needs this containment around it? What are they trying to stop that she's doing in this thing that I'm studying—black women writers and women writers, and how often that comes up, that writing on the wall?

Up until the election I was like o*h, okay, let me discipline my way of speaking so that people can understand what I'm saying so they don't think that I'm crazy*—and I'm talking about the sight and all of that. That shit is over. No, I know things. The things that I know are acceptable forms of knowledge, and I'm out there just saying the stuff that I know now instead of trying to fit things into this molded way of being that has never made any sense anyway.

That way of approaching the election is leading me to think about the things that we do write down and how we write them down, and living in the impossible and making the history of that a visible thing instead of being like, *These are the ways we're supposed to have these conversations. This is whose fault Trump is. This is whose fault this is. This stuff is happening.*

No. I don't believe in the system. The system has always been nonsense, because all the system has ever said to me is, "You don't exist." And I'm like, "But I be right here." Again, that way of talking is just disciplining us into certain ruts so that we have the same conversation over and over again in a way that I'm just not interested in. I'm much more interested now in different forms of knowledge and how they work and how we express them to people and where that gets us...That's where I am on the whole Trump thing.

SH: When people feel abandoned by their representatives, they always turn to their artists, so do you feel that responsibility as an artist? You [both] write about big issues—you're writing about gender and race and class and religion. Do you feel compelled to do that? Do you do it just because that's what you care about, and do you feel responsibility to do that as an artist?

LVC-S: I do. Terrance Hayes has a line in one of his poems ["Lighthead's Guide to the Galaxy"] where he's talking about the way his father speaks: *I'd rather have what my daddy calls / "skrimp." He says "discrete" and means the street / just out of sight.*

I'm always telling my students, "I'm writing for that street. That street right there. Discrete." That's where I'm trying to get to and bump all this other stuff...I feel like it's imperative to just call bullshit on these models at this point. I'm done with doing it in the way that it's supposed to be done. Like, if you're going to write about race, or if you're going to write about gender, or if you're going to write about any of these things, *these are the ways that you have to do it.* And instead be like, *oh yeah, skrimp and discrete,* you know? I want all of the stuff that's in there. I want the mass in there. What are the equations that go with that skrimp and discrete, and how do I follow that and write open intervals and really start to comment about thinking?

This is the way that my mind actually works—instead of *this is the way that your mind is supposed to work.* [I want to] just follow that—*follow those portals* is the way I think about them. How do we get through those spaces so that we can get somewhere, instead of spinning around in a circle all the time, saying the same things in the same way, so that the system that grinds us up can just grind us up, and then grind up a new generation and a new generation?

RGH: Let me ask you a question. I have felt a very powerful impatience since the advent of us giving Trump so much power. Was that the feeling you were referring to when you say *I'm done now*? Is that the now?

LVC-S: Yeah. I'm saying for so long, "Here's a thing that's going to happen. It's happening. It's happening. It's happening." And everybody's telling me, "The thing that you're saying is going to happen is impossible. We have pundits, we have number counters, we have crunchers. They're saying it's not gonna happen." And I'm saying, "You are wrong." And they're saying, "How do you know?" And I'm like, "'Cause my mama had the sight, my great-grandmama had the sight, and I have it, too." And then instead of dismissing that, thinking, *What does that mean? Why could my great-grandmama see things? Why can my mama see things? How am I able to see things?*

I'm tying that back into what I do, so that I'm thinking of it more and more now as a type of close reading. I'm a really good close reader. I can close read the hell out of some stuff because if I didn't when I was a child, bad shit was going to happen if I didn't close read the situation. How is the sight a type of close reading that people then should acknowledge as a type of close reading, you know? Where does it come from, and how can we then use that to get us out of some of the situations that we're in?

RGH: I haven't addressed this publicly, but I will because I, too, have felt the last straw for me was giving [Trump] the keys to our kingdom. [In] the spring of 2016 I was diagnosed with cancer, but before I got my diagnosis, I had been reading a lot of Audre Lorde, because I was coming here [to Berea College] and she was on my heart to [give] to the students. Lorde had loosened her tongue upon her [own] cancer diagnosis. That was her moment of *I understand now that there is no time left for bullshit.*

I did not connect those events when I got my diagnosis. I just went into panic and then went into surgery after surgery after surgery. I'm fine now, but it was in the midst of those surgeries that [Donald Trump was elected]. When that season came upon me, I had my Audre Lorde moment of *oh, right, there is absolutely no time to waste.*

Art is many things to many people, and I'm not going to be the person who says art can only be this thing, but for me, it is my practice of prayer, it is my practice of seeking truth. And maybe because my daddy was a Marine, maybe because bad things would happen if I wasn't paying close enough attention as a kid, I am obsessively watching—or, I should say, reading—all the time, so I can't help but now have it all in my work. Pretending like it's not on my mind is not going to do anymore...There's no time now to not say whatever you've got in you to say, what you know to be true.

LVC-S: It's funny that you bring up Audre Lorde with that because, also back in 2013, I got really sick. The worst of it was that I woke up one day and my right leg was paralyzed. I went to the emergency room, and my best friends were with me...I had an MRI. I got back a test result from the hospital that had on [it]: "likely due to the patient's wig."

This is the hair that grows out of my head; there are no extensions on my head. I went into the hospital with a paralyzed leg. They gave me a diagnosis that said, *That can't possibly be your real hair.* And I thought, *why in the world would I continue to listen and discipline my own thought processes and the way I think and everything in this system that is set up—where I'm meant to say, this is empirical science, and we know a thing, and we're going to tell you about your body.* With everything Miss Audre is writing in the cancer diaries where she's like, *I'm not believing anything these people tell me about my body. They're not living in my body. Until I feel this, this, and this, she told herself, then I'm not buying any of it.*

After I [got] back [the] MRI result, that happened in me, too, where I'm just like, *I do not have to be in any way engaged with this system in the way that people say that I have to engage with it. I do not have to be polite about that either because this is some nonsense.*

SH: Audre Lorde, if I'm not mistaken...called that unsilencing "the transformation of beauty into action." I love that idea of beauty in action and that writing can result in those two things.

RGH: I don't know what the responsibility of other artists is, but I know what my responsibility as a citizen is, and I just happen to also be an artist. What is it like for you? What's your answer?

SH: Well, that's exactly my answer. I don't have a judgment for artists that don't do that, but I feel like I don't have a choice in the matter. I feel like I have to say something. Sometimes I wish I wasn't that way, you know?

RGH Well, it doesn't make you popular. I don't know what it's like for you, but I know as a woman that if you speak your mind, you're angry and a bitch.

LVC-S: And a diva.

RGH: One thing I'm meditating on right now in the poems I'm working on is that we are in this cacophony of noise, but it's all a repetition, too. It's this absolute chaos that's made of repeated ways of saying and thinking. I find my peace when I pull back into bell hooks's work or Wendell Berry's work—people who have the imaginative and intellectual prowess to reframe. Every time I watch Wendell in an essay make a move, he's making a move to reframe. He pulls back. He offers another frame. I don't have that prowess yet, but I want to be in its company.

LVC-S: You were saying something [to me] earlier [in conversation] about your process that I thought was so important and so interesting—that you approach your writing as a listener. I think that's so important, and I'm doing the same thing. Lucille Clifton had that poem ["why some people be mad at me sometimes"] where she says, *they ask me to remember / but they want me to remember / their memories / and I keep on remembering / mine.* I'm trying to remember things that they say it's not possible for us to remember...I feel like words have power in them. How do we get there? Part of that is writing into the silence with that ear attuned for *am I gonna hear this voice? Is it gonna come through? What is it gonna say?* Not *I'm gonna say this thing that people are not saying is smart for people like me.* ■

HILLBILLY TRANSPLANT: PONDERING PARK DOMINOES AND THE DEATH OF CELIA CRUZ

July 16, 2003

In other places, slick, smooth plastic clatter
across family formica tables,
bright white bars and black divots
so round and perfect they might hold
plump orange caviar, a smattering
of pepper and sea salt,
or seat for pungent capers.
But across the burroughs,
in Far Rockaway, Bensonhurst, Washington Heights,
Saturday streets smell of sweet onions,
barbacoa, huancaina, the parks
with their chess tables convert to dominoes,
old Dominican men and Eastern European boys
sit to a game, pieces move in careful
patterns, groups of men on either side
sweat and chatter and gesture.
No language barrier, they speak in forehead slaps
of flawed moves, claps on the back when it's well done.
Plates of grilled vegetables, brick oven breads
and meats spiced from oceans apart passed
around both sides of the table bring fingers to lips,
groans of appreciation.

There is no shared language for grief,
but there is food, so plates of ropa vieja,

rice and sofrito are laid across the tables,
dominoes put away, heads nod, hips salsa
as Celia Cruz's smoky voice carries from speakers
across the parks, from parked cars lining Lenox Avenue,
air split with timbale and great belling brass notes,
and even the youngest of European boys grins
and finds the words *La Negra Tiene Tumbao,*
the old Ukrainian men shout *Azucár!*
and grasp the forearms of the Cubans,
cheering them when the dominoes
are brought back out, smacking their lips
in approval as they move pieces, clack
and clatter lifting again beneath guitar and claves.

LISA J. PARKER

HILLBILLY TRANSPLANT: WORKING AT THE METROPOLITAN OPERA

First month, I run my hands against those burgundy,
crushed velvet walls lined with portraits of Caruso and Callas,
swoon when Placido Domingo holds the elevator for me,
and again when I hear the early rehearsal for *La Boheme*
through the old RCA speaker perched on a shelf in my office.

Second month, I invent errands to run,
lose myself to the maze of hallways beneath the stage.
Something akin to *Alice In Wonderland*, each hall
is shorter than the next, the ceiling lower and lower
until the giant coffin-sized case of a symphony bass
has to stand at a pitch, propped sideways against a piano
just to fit. Each hall lined with racks of costumes
seems stranger than the next, Verdi-inspired props, a huge
bird costume from *The Marriage of Figaro*, ballerinas
from the Bolshoi scatter at my footfall, exit a side room
toward me, a billow of contraband smoke rushing
out from behind them. They wear heated slippers,
legwarmers that accentuate their heart-shaped calves.

Third month, I ponder the $7 cafeteria clamshell
of mostly arugula and tiny scoop of tuna, wonder
how close I am to maxing out that last card, how much
we could save in rent if we called the walled-off part
of our living room a bedroom, sell some other artist
the dream of living on Broadway, neglect to mention
the subway directly under us or the projects on Amsterdam
on the other side of the block. Finish tuna while listening

to stagehands and set designers talk union politics.
Make grocery list, wonder how far $40 will stretch, wonder
how many bags I can carry the six blocks from Gristedes
back to the apartment. Wonder if it will rain on me.

Fourth month, tally two-year debt, take lunch
in my office, skip cafeteria, skip courtyard performance
of Juilliard musicians, turn dial of my RCA speaker to *off*
when the soft tremolo mandolin of Don Giovanni
leaves me hand-over-mouth crying,
a barrage of homesick images: family reunions,
great uncles plucking mandolins cradled on their broad chests,
picking guitars, banjos, everyone foundering
in lawn chairs in that pressing Virginia heat,
pregnant, always, with rain and threat of storm.
No amount of staring out the floor to ceiling window
at the grand fountain or City Ballet in Lincoln Square
can disenthrone those faces or voices, singing
mountain ballads, hymns, and Stanley Brothers standards,
sweaty hands clasped, voices perfectly imperfect,
soul-savingly beautiful, my heart's familiar redemption.
I know as sure as I've known anything here,
that I will leave this city and its grandeur, return South,
settle in a tree-laden space with mountains around me
and no doubt dream of crushed velvet walls
and halls filled with bel canto runs and ballerinas.

LISA J. PARKER

CLEAVE

The world makes no distinction
between the knife that parts the wall
or sorts the army your heart has built,
or the one that makes room and way
for love, that open space we fill with nights
by the creek or sprawled on quilts
to watch the Perseids fall above us.
It makes no distinction
between *that* knife and the one that will
draw open miles of vascular roads
that wind from heart to wrist or what
you want to spill to the earth like dust
from that box, from that pewter box
to slick river-grassed water, the knife
that parts the water around rock and stump
and sycamore rise, around heron's legs
and a hundred years of leaf rot
or the rock that covers our wedding bands
where I tied them together and pushed them
in a birch leaf beneath the sulphur-marked stone
beneath a split trunk poplar whose lean
shelters all the shaded things we sat beneath and in.
The world makes no distinction one knife
to another, it cuts the same direction,
same depth to open for entry as it does
to open for all that will spill and fall
and be dashed against rock and river.

LISA J. PARKER

PASSING OF GRIEF

Your desert boots in the corner of the closet,
slump against hardwood where you left them by the door,
where I left them by the door, that cracking sound
they made when lifted from that hard, still place,
something giving way.

Canoe through Shenandoah current where
river is just river and sun on my shoulders
a reminder of all that bears down to grow
the green of sycamores and sassafras to shade
and tame heat that bounces back off water
I rest my fingers against, silken tangle
through skeins of river grass you may
have settled against when we scattered you here,
all the inlet shrubs, white ash and sugar maples,
all the herons' nests you might have wound yourself into,
or tiny moving things you might be bone or scale
or wing of now.

Canoe tied to the truck roof myself,
knots of rope I have learned these last years,
air filter I can pull from my engine, replace
with a snap and four clicks, sound
of the truck hood slamming shut,
everything beneath it a steady hum.

LISA J. PARKER

CIRCULATION

JON SEALY

Booth Chandler still thought of the *Issaqueena Star* as his newspaper even though he'd long since sold it to the assholes in Virginia—and grown rich and fat in the process. Now he had an opportunity to become some kind of executive with our parent company, which I'd been waiting for him to do for ten years. I wanted his job as publisher, but my prospects were in real doubt.

"I've been rubbing elbows with the executives," Booth said to me after he returned to South Carolina. He pronounced it *ex-ZEH-cutives*. "Yes, sir, rubbing elbows." He snapped his suspenders, a piece of apparel he'd been wearing for the past forty years and hadn't needed in at least twenty. These days he was lucky the elastic in those suckers could stretch the girth of him.

"Say you have?" I said. "You going to take a position up there?"

"You trying to get rid of me?"

"Wouldn't dream of it. Just dreaming about being publisher one day, when it's my time."

"If I recommended you as my replacement," he said.

"I haven't failed you yet," I said, thinking of a warehouse full of *It's the Holidays!* magazine, which I thought of as *Buy! Buy! Buy!*, our annual spam-in-print advertising section where we coerced every retailer in the Foothills to participate or risk being shut out to consumers. We never would have put out such schlock on our own, but to our parent company, which as far as I could tell was run by a bunch of illiterate snake-oil salesmen looking to line their pockets at the expense of their employees and shareholders, we didn't produce journalism. We manufactured content.

We would be shipping the magazine out with the paper in a few weeks. Trouble was: while he'd been hobnobbing with the board of directors in Virginia last week, I'd accidentally added an extra zero to the order and bought 100,000 of the suckers, ten times our circulation. It should have been proofread—I should have proofread it.

"You're a good man, Lucky, I'll give you that." Booth took his chin in his hand—and there was a lot of chin to grab hold of—and frowned. "You know I've been here all my life, just about."

"Richmond's a fine city," I said. "Good restaurants. Good economy. Good place to retire."

"They do have a race track," he said. "The executives took me out to the races on Friday. You ever been to NASCAR?"

"I've been to some stock car races," I said. "When I was a kid."

"I don't know about stock cars, but NASCAR is something else. When those cars come around the track, you can feel it something fierce up in your spine. And when they wreck—BAMBOO!"

Booth meant to say *ka-BOOM*. One day he told us he was excited to have ordered our photographer a new telepathic lens for his camera. Lately, he'd taken to drinking that Firefly vodka with lemonade, and when he made them he would say, "It's time for a Tom Arnold." We never corrected him.

"Sounds like you had a blast up there."

"You've been up there. You know. Them executives are swarming. You got to be serious about business to make it up there."

This from a man who once delivered mimeographed newspapers on a bicycle while high on mescaline. I could see him slapping papers against mailboxes and yelling: BAMBOO!

■ ■ ■

Forty-some-odd years after starting the *Star*, Booth still strutted the halls, his shirt buttons popping off if he stretched the wrong way, and I was doing everything I could to keep our budget under control and to keep our six-person operation as efficient as could be considering the newspaper business was under assault from Wall Street, shareholders, Amazon, Facebook, Twitter, Apple, Madison Avenue, bloggers, aggregators, thieves, hustlers, scam artists, and every office of government between here and the U.S. Capitol.

In addition to Booth (our publisher) and me (our operations manager), we had in the office: Constance McNally, our proofreader/traffic manager/customer service representative/IT specialist (even though we didn't have a website, or even an Internet connection in the office, someone had to repair the fax machine and the printers); Jerry Pickens, our graphic designer/business office manager/delivery boy; Grudge Sorrells, our reporter/senior editor/photographer/circulation manager/groundskeeper; and Ashley Shark, who sold all our advertising and who, I'm sure, would soon leave us to go sell medical supplies down in Anderson, or even, God help her, pharmaceuticals over in Greenville.

Unlike Booth Chandler or Ashley Shark, who each had an escape hatch, I was locked into the job—not just for the money, which was laughable, but because it gave my life a semblance of purpose. My wife and I couldn't have children, which we said was fine even though it was not. She had her career as an oncologist, which had taken ten years of college, and what they didn't tell my generation when they told us to focus on our careers is that conception grows complicated in your thirties. We've lived longer than Jesus, and our bodies aren't what they used to be. If we were factories, we'd have a few snags on the assembly line, which meant no children unless we adopted. Between the two of us we still had a mortgage's worth of student loans, so we enjoyed the company of our two over-fed and under-exercised dogs, Flip and Flop. Not a bad life from the outside, overall, though some days, I'll admit, I did want to drive my pickup into a ravine just to get my blood circulating again.

The day after Booth returned from Virginia, and he told his tales of meeting the executives, he went to his office and closed the door. We wouldn't see him for the rest of the day—I don't know if he was drinking, or napping, or shopping eBay for a bargain.

I poured a cup of rancid coffee and walked over to the traffic desk where Constance was reading over tomorrow's Schools section. She was tall and wore boots and could spell anything in the dictionary, it seemed: bizarre, bazaar, lizard, blizzard. *Hors d'oeuvres.* ("Whores devour," I always had to say to remember the V came before the R.) She spent a good hour each night proofreading obituaries, making sure World War III vets weren't scheduled for internment.

"Anything good in the old textbook loony bin?" I said.

"There's an outbreak of meningitis over in Easley," she said. "The governor's using it as a reason to up her stance for abstinence education. She's releasing a statement at noon today."

"What does meningitis have to do with abstinence?"

"What does my keychain have to do with the gold standard? These people are crazy," she said, kicking her boots rhythmically against the desk as she spoke. "Do you know what we're seeing on the wire? Up in Virginia the state legislature is on an all-out war against Planned Parenthood. How long do you think it will be before Roe v. Wade is overturned? All that work they did in the '60s and '70s—gone. This is South Carolina, so you know we'll be leading the charge. If the governor had her way, she'd have me chained to a kitchenette with four babies at my feet—never mind that all of them would be on food stamps and Medicaid and what that would do to the state budget."

"Whoa now," I said. I didn't say how my mother was one of those women from the '70s who protested this or that and maybe burned her bra. I didn't say how my mother today was, maybe, a Democrat but cautiously married to my father, a lifelong Republican, both of them now conservative rascals who just wanted to keep their AARP-lobbied-for government benefits. I didn't say, "I sympathize with you, Constance, but, you know, I'm suspicious of activism of any kind. Hey, what would you do if all was well and you didn't have a cause that needed to be fought for? You'd hang yourself out of boredom. Trust me, I know." Instead, what I said was: "Looks like a good B section."

Constance, who was near tears, nodded.

"We got some good art for this week in Sports," Grudge said from a few desks down. "After Seneca whooped up on us last Friday, Coach Scooter set the team to running laps for three hours every afternoon, so the front page is an aerial of the field with the players doing sprints."

"Sounds like a good one," I said. "Hey, let me ask you this." I walked over to Grudge, leaving Constance to kick her boots by herself. She was already hunched over the page again, gaping fish-eyed at too-small font. I said to Grudge: "Hey, what's our circulation like these days?"

"Holding steady. You know that." He looked up at me over his glasses with beady, bloodshot eyes. Those were the eyes of a hawk-keen reporter who smelled blood.

I poured a cup of rancid coffee and walked over to the traffic desk where Constance was reading over tomorrow's Schools section.

"That's what I figured," I said, stalling.

He set his pen down and leaned back in his chair. "Why, what's on your mind?"

"You know any way to perhaps increase our circulation by tenfold?"

Grudge laughed. Constance nearby and even Jerry and Ashley across the room all started laughing as well.

"Just a thought," I said.

I walked toward the side door of the building, which led out to the loading dock. Grudge followed, and when the two of us were out there he shook a cigarette out of his pack and fired one up. Grudge had about twenty-five years on me, a veteran newsman stuck in Issaqueena County, though perhaps he'd say he was happy to be here. He never went to college, never had the kind of opportunities Booth and I had, but he'd also never had to work in the cotton mills like my father and Booth's family and just about everyone else in Issaqueena who didn't work for Duke Power.

Our town straddled Lake Hartwell about fifteen miles off I-85 west of Greenville. Clemson University was one town over, and we lived in the shadow of the mountains. That combination—Greenville and the university and the mountains—made for an interesting clash of cultures. Our local tavern was the Boathouse, and on any given night you might find some shaggy Communist professor drinking craft beer to chase away the high lonesome, a group of bluegrass playing mountain bikers, and a couple of good-old-boy teenagers with fake IDs. That was Grudge's crowd—he played bass in band called Bobcat Fangs. I envied him that. He never met a stranger, and if he did he'd fight him outside the bar then buy him a beer afterward. That's how male friendships seemed to work: fight, then friends. I'd never been in a fight, and didn't have enough male friends.

A few miles away from the Boathouse, you have a few neighborhoods of Greenville businessmen and their realtor housewives, the men oblivious to the true nature of the town where they lived. They were from foreign lands such as Ohio, and we were their bedroom community. I knew those men, because as operations manager for the paper, I was always trying to cook up some new business deal, to get their money and Greenville-clout to participate in our local wheeling and dealing. Many of them subscribed to our paper, but sent their children to private schools elsewhere. On occasion, I got out on the golf course with them and managed not to slice it too badly. But in the end I was unsuccessful with my infiltration efforts. The *Star* was local yokel for life, it seemed.

I exchanged a few pleasantries with Grudge on the loading dock. College football, another local business shutting its doors, our respective families. Grudge had three grown children, a bicycle, and his bluegrass buddies, so his life was jam-packed with entertainment, with purpose. I'm sure he never had trouble falling asleep at night.

He flicked his cigarette off the dock and said, finally: "You worried about our circulation numbers?"

"Should I be?"

"Not on my end. Look at these boxes." He pointed to the boxes with 100,000 copies of *It's the Holidays!* and said, "That's enough subscribers to pay for my retirement, assuming Booth didn't just sell us all out in Virginia. I just wondered if you knew something I didn't."

"You mean from the board of directors, plans for our paper?" I said. "Booth didn't tell me anything, but he would have if something were going down."

"They're shutting down papers all over for no reason. We should never have gone public, never should have let those weasels take us over," he said. "I'm about old enough to retire, so if the end is coming, you don't have to worry about shielding me. Constance is the only one I'd worry about breaking the news to."

"What? Grudge. There's no news."

"I'll just take my pension and freelance, maybe for the *Independent*, or even the *Greenville News*."

"But we need you here, buddy. You don't have to be plotting out your retirement just yet."

"Maybe I'll even take a trip. They're giving us a buy-out, I presume? Some kind of severance?"

"No, no severance. You're staying here. We're staying open."

"I'm going to miss this place," he said, and he turned to go inside. I didn't stop him. I figured he would sit down and go back to work, that he didn't actually believe we were on the verge of insolvency. He was wrong about any news from Virginia, but, as I looked at the holiday boxes, ten times the number that should have come in, I wondered if we had enough cash reserves to cover it. I ran the numbers here, so it occurred to me that if I could get Booth to take that job up in Virginia, to join the ranks of the executives, I could pull some accounting trick to make these extras disappear over the next few years.

I hopped off the loading dock and pulled my pickup around and, quick as a mischievous hound can scarf up some holiday cookies left out to cool, I counted out a tenth of the holiday guide shipment and began loading the rest into the bed of my truck. This would take a few trips. I had no idea what ninety thousand magazines looked like. How did the state papers manage such volume? The shocks bottomed out and the bed hung low over the pavement. I got in and had to rev the engine something fierce to get going. Truck squeaking like a nonplussed cricket, I rolled away and parked down the street, out of sight of the paper's office. No one in town would bother with the boxes in my truck. So long as I could made about a dozen trips like this, I was home free.

■ ■ ■

"That's right, there's about 300 of these boxes," I said over the phone. "I don't know for how long. Couple of months maybe."

I looked up and tipped over backward in my chair when I saw Booth standing in my office. For such a fat fellow he was remarkably light-footed. He stood there with a report in his hand and seemed in no hurry for me to get off the phone.

"Hello? Hello?" said a man through the receiver.

I groaned and scrambled up and picked up the receiver. Booth stared at me with a curious gleam, like I was some kind of baboon in a magic show. BAMBOO!

"Sorry about that," I said to the storage operator. "I'll be there after work today with my first load."

When I hung up, Booth asked if everything were all right.

"Just moving some stuff into storage," I said.

"Ah." He nodded. "How's your wife doing?"

"What? She's fine."

"The economy the way it's been this year, the recovery not taking off, I know it's hard times."

Booth sat in the chair across from me. He set the report on the corner of my desk and squinted at me.

"I know it's tough—it's tough on all of us—but if you're having trouble at home, if you need to take some time to work on your marriage—"

"No, no, nothing like that," I said. "I've just got some old athletic equipment I want to clear out of the garage." I hadn't owned any athletic equipment since I was a teenager. You wouldn't know it, because I'm trim, but I don't do physical activity. So why say athletic equipment? Who knows why things pop into our minds at a moment's notice. Neurons zip around up there like bingo balls, and maybe there's no order to the world at all, just random strikes of lightning.

"Not my business," Booth went on, "but I remember when y'all found out you couldn't have children. I remember Cindy at that year's Christmas party."

"She's fine, Booth. She's working too much, but she's fine."

"It's true, children enrich your life, but a marriage is about more than procreation."

"In fact we're looking at a trip over the holidays, taking a weekend in Kiawah."

"You have to work at it, son."

"Did you need something? What you got there?" I said.

"I know a good counselor, if you need it," Booth said. Then he picked up the report and handed it over. "This is just something I came across in my travels. Thought you might like to take a look."

"Thanks, Booth." I took the report, a survey from the Virginia Press Association about how mobile advertising had overtaken digital or something. Booth was always delivering me useless reports that I don't think he read or understood himself, and I don't know what he wanted me to do with them. He might follow up in six weeks and ask how our mobile

Booth still had a landline at his house and still thought a fax machine was the latest and greatest. A 1970s progressive in the 2010s.

advertising efforts were going. Booth still had a landline at his house and still thought a fax machine was the latest and greatest. A 1970s progressive in the 2010s.

"You let me know if you and Cindy need some time," he said.

■ ■ ■

That evening I sent an unanswered text to Cindy, letting her know I'd be late, then I drove out to the U-Store-It on Highway 123. There was a Hardee's next door and a cemetery and an apartment complex across the street. Daylight savings ended last month so dusk settled in as I left work. I drove through the twilight and pulled into the storage center at full dark. There, a squat young fellow with a runny red nose and leaking eyeballs met me at the front entrance.

"I called earlier," I said. "About the boxes."

"Oh right." He sniffled, then looked in the back of my truck. The dude was maybe twenty, had shaggy blonde hair and was weighted down with what I took to be video-game fat. I imagined he didn't do much but eat and watch television and maybe smoke pot. His immune system was under assault from grease and lethargy—hence the wet nose. "You from the paper?" he said.

"That's right, the *Issaqueena Star*."

"My parents read that," he said. "Hey, how's Booth Chandler doing?"

"He's OK. You know him?"

"My uncle plays golf with him. Is that what all these boxes are about?"

"I'm just using boxes from the office. This is some personal stuff."

"Lot of it," Leaky Dude said. He stared gape-jawed at the twenty boxes weighing down the bed of my truck. "That'll fit in one unit, though."

"Actually, I've got about ten batches of these."

He blinked a few times and made me wonder if he was one of those vaccination-autistic kids you hear about. I was only thirty-five, which isn't old anymore, but there was a serious gulf between me and kids even ten years younger. Their brains didn't work right, and more than once I'd wondered what it would have been like to raise a child in such a world. Maybe it was a good thing, for the grand social good, not to bring more people into what was surely a self-destructive species.

He led me to an empty unit and together we unloaded the holiday guide boxes. I was glad Leaky Dude didn't seem to notice—or didn't care—that these boxes were still sealed and had the *Star* address label on them. Someone less oblivious might have wondered how I managed to seal personal things in unwrapped boxes, but Leaky Dude must have been high on Ritalin or Percocet or Paxil or Aderoll or Zoloft or Zyco-what's-it that's all the rage these days, that helps the kids keep from shooting each other in the legs just to feel something.

When the boxes were in the unit we stared at them for a moment, and Leaky Dude seemed to be counting and making calculations.

"You got a tape measure?" I asked. "Never mind. Hey, this doesn't look too bad. Rent me out two for now and I'll make it work."

Leaky Dude blinked a few times, then agreed.

Two hours later, the U-Store-It office was closed and I was on my last batch of boxes from the paper. The shocks on my pickup must have been shot by this point. The poor thing groaned just from sitting empty and untouched in the parking lot.

I stacked the last box in the unit, then turned and, for the second time that day, fell over from surprise.

"What are you doing?" asked Constance McNally, who for some reason stood over me, still in her boots, towering. Her hair had frizzed out, for it was a moist night, and she looked like a crazy lady with wild eyes and a maniacal grin.

"Shit, Constance." I sat up and brushed rock bits off my elbows. I could feel bruises and fabric burns on my skin. "What are you doing here?"

She blushed. "The lease on my apartment is up. I'm trying to close on a house, but the house didn't make the appraisal, and the seller won't come down in price."

"So you're living in a storage unit?"

"No," she nearly yelled. "I moved back in with my parents and rented a unit to store some furniture."

Constance was around thirty. I didn't ask what it was like to move back in with your parents at that age. When I visited my parents a few towns over, I felt tall and clunky in their house. I think marriage is what started it. You take on a family of your own, and suddenly your old homestead is no longer yours. You become a guest like everyone else. Constance had never been married and, as far as I could tell, didn't have a boyfriend. She was nice looking but she could appear demented after having her head too deep in proofreading. Eyes crinkled. Capillaries burst.

I reached up and pulled the door of my storage unit down.

"Are those boxes from the office?" she asked.

I brought some boxes home the other day. Got a few things I want to store myself."

"I'll say," she said.

Had she seen the boxes were still sealed in their original packing tape? Leaky Dude missed it, but Constance was trained to noticc small details. Use a single space between sentences. En dashes versus em dashes versus hyphens. Whores devour. I could see her tomorrow, huddled next to Grudge on the smoking ramp, staring at the remaining copies of *It's the Holidays!* and agonizing over what she should do. "It's going to come out regardless," Grudge would say with the flick of his cigarette, and then, surveying the loading dock with the look of a man who knows he's wasted his life and the resignation of one who understands there's nothing he can do to fix it, he would add, "Best thing either of us can do is get our resumes out there." Maybe Constance would march into Booth's office and disillusion him of any further big meetings with the ex-ZEH-cutives, or maybe she would go back to her desk, eye me furtively, and freshen up her slender resume, which would be blessedly free of typos at least. Maybe Booth would call me into the office and see on my face the truth, that I had made a business-busting error. What could be said?

"What are you up to now?" I asked Constance tonight.

"I'm meeting some friends for a drink."

"The Boathouse?"

"No, we're going over to a friend's apartment," she said with the upward lilt of invitation.

Even if I found some way of fixing the error and keeping us out of bankruptcy, Booth would likely take the position in Virginia, clearing the way for me to move up to publisher. No manager needs to be caught with a drink around his employee, not anymore. I heard the stories of the *Star*'s old days—bottles hidden in walls, mimosas par for the course, pools, horses, reckless driving. Booth and Grudge were the only ones left from those days, bodies no doubt preserved after being soaked in so much alcohol. I told her I'd see her tomorrow, and then I watched her walk off and get into a vehicle shaped like a shoe. She motored onto the highway and her taillights faded in the night. I locked the storage unit and tried not to consider what it would mean when the truth about the magazines came out. For now, I enjoyed the rush that comes with urgencies. I would go home and try to make love to my wife, if she were home and would have me. And if not? If not, there was one more uncertainty in the growing list of unknowns. ■

TONIC EXORCISM

Knees grown weak from kneeling, tongues weary
of even the most basic prayer, they turned
to Clayton who said he had a tonic for anything,
especially the demons that bore inside
the child like weevils, moved her limbs wildly
in the middle of the night. Done-in by the screaming,
her parents acquiesced, and so brought Clayton
to their barn where the horses crowded the shadows
of their stalls, neighed amongst themselves
in the frightened beast-talk even the people
had learned to speak, watched as the child
was held down in straw the color of lanterns
that once freed this place of darkness.
Her legs pinned, they moved quickly, motioned
to Clayton who pulled from his coat a bottle
stronger than any bible verse, the liquid primordial
in its blackness, poured it deep inside the child
until her body smoothed like a pond on the edge of winter,
until her parents relaxed their grips on her arms, gave
    Clayton
ten dollars for doing what the priest could not.
If it took the drink, so be it, they said as night turned cool
and they made plans to buy as many bottles
as they could, vowing never to be surprised
by any demon or fallow field again, realizing then,
as they all would that winter in Boone,
what scripture could do and what it could not.

JOSHUA LEE MARTIN

CUTTING

In the afternoons the boy fumbles with the hatchet
like the razor he took from his father

the day he wanted to shave the child
off of his face. From my porch I watch

him swing into a pitch pine at the edge
of his field, its yellow flesh chipping

with each hack, the gouge now the size
of his thin wrists. Because he is not my son

I do not gently place my hands on his shoulders,
show him how to angle the blade

so that the trunk will fall in the direction of his anger.
Because he is not my son I do not tell him

what I think his cutting means, do not point
across the field to where, miles away,

a highway snakes down this mountain,
past the wilted crops and merciless churches,

past his father whisky-waltzing down
the dirt drive with a woman

who's not his mother, past the kitchens stuffed
with bowls of cold rice and butter. Instead I sit

and watch his strokes fall harder the moment
his father kicks the front door open, screams *boy,*

get the hell in here, the rusted edge
of his voice slashing through the wind.

JOSHUA LEE MARTIN

TRUTH AND CONSEQUENCES: ON WRITING AND NOT WRITING POETRY

PAULETTA HANSEL

From this vantage point, the ten-year silence in my writing life, from my mid-twenties until my mid-thirties, no longer seems particularly important. Or rather, it seems as if it should not be. I am in my late fifties. I have been writing again for longer than I stopped, for longer than what I've called my first writing life, which began in my early teens and ended with that silence. Since age thirty-five, I have published six books of poems, have poetry and prose in several journals, written and performed a one-woman play, carved out a meager living as a creative writing teacher, and earned an MFA. But I cannot write about this abundance without addressing the silence, the negative space in my life with words.

I began writing poetry when so many girls begin, at age thirteen when there is simply nothing else to do with all of that. When I was not writing, I was crying, though nothing in particular was wrong, then, in my life. I oozed adolescent angst. It had to go somewhere; it might as well be on the page.

Do I exaggerate? Of course I exaggerate. I was thirteen.

But I am not exaggerating when I say that no one—not my parents nor their friends, not my peers nor teachers—related to me as if I were thirteen. I looked older. I spoke older. I read older, jumping quickly over the "Young Adult" section of the local library in my small Appalachian town into the 19th Century Romantics in the library of the college where my father taught. Only my heart was thirteen, but that was not obvious from the physical and intellectual package.

Within a year, I embarked upon a "relationship" with a man ten years my senior; my poems no longer cried out for a nameless, formless love, but chronicled an emotionally abusive relationship which I longed to transform into true love or, at least, to maintain. Within two years, I was a published poet, first through Scholastic's national high school competition and then in some of the new Appalachian literary journals. I traveled to conferences and participated in readings with writers my parents' age. Within three years, I was included in a feature article in *Ms. Magazine* as an up-and-coming Appalachian woman writer.

And woven into that brief autobiography: anorexia, promiscuity, alcohol abuse, depression.

Throughout all of that, I kept writing, though the "I" in those lyric poems I wrote bears little resemblance to the self I now remember. The picture that emerges from those poems is that of a young woman who is operating from a core of strength and self-sufficiency and whom you know will emerge largely unscathed from the chaos of which she writes.

I was not that girl. She was my mask.

■ ■ ■

Former poet laureate Billy Collins is a strong proponent of the "poet as persona" theory, having said, "[T]he important breakthrough moment for a poet is when he or she has developed a kind of character through which he or she can speak with ease. This character—or persona—resembles the poet in many ways but is clearly a refinement of the actual person."[1]

During those prolific years of my first writing life this is exactly what I was doing—unconsciously, perhaps, and certainly without ever having heard the advice of the not-yet poet laureate, I had created a persona from which I could stand at some distance from my life. And this was a logical, even laudable progression for me as a young writer; my poetry had climbed up out of the primordial ooze into something more crafted, literary. My persona (I named her "the lady") allowed me Wordsworth's "emotion recollected in tranquility" in order to write and revise increasingly mature poems.[2] But like the rest of my life at that time, this maturity, this

1 Billy Collins. "A Conversation with James Mustich." *Barnes and Noble Review,* December 1, 2008.

2 William Wordsworth. "Preface to *Lyrical Ballads, with Pastoral and Other Poems* (1802)." *The Norton Anthology of English Literature.* Ed. Stephen Greenblatt et al. Vol. 2., 8th ed. (New York: Norton, 2006).

temporary distance from the muddled reality of my life, was too much, too soon.

■ ■ ■

"Poetry found me. / It almost saved me. / It was not enough." This stanza from my poem, *Curriculum Vitae 2005,* is about these early writing years. When I wrote the poem I had not yet read Gregory Orr's book, *Poetry as Survival.* "At some point in prehistory," Orr writes, "human culture developed the personal lyric so that imagination would have another way of assisting the individual self to cope. When someone, in the throes of a powerful and disturbing experience, turns instinctively to the writing or reading of a poem, it is because they sense the personal lyric can be a powerful aid in helping them survive and make sense of their experience."[3]

My impulse as a young writer was toward poetry as a healing force, first as a girl trying to make sense of her emotional and physical transformation, and later as a young woman whose early sexual involvement with an immature, abusive adult led to a myriad of physical and emotional challenges. (Even now, I hide this girl behind those distancing words. The truth is I tried to starve myself back into prepubescence. I slept with anyone who asked. I binge drank to numb my despair.) Poetry was not, in fact, enough of tool: not a wide-enough shield, not a sharp-enough sword. With my writing persona I created armor to attempt to address the disorder of my young life. But while the persona allowed such order on the page, it prevented much of the healing that

3 Gregory Orr. *Poetry as Survival.* (Athens: University of Georgia Press, 2002), 22.

poetry could have bestowed. Poetry as truth telling. Poetry to reveal self to self. Poetry as claiming the worthiness of self. It is hard for me to reconcile these two girls—the one whose poems I still have, and the one whose photo is propped up by the window as I write these words. She is too thin, though she doesn't know it. She is wearing a T-shirt she stole from a store at the Mall. She is fifteen—just—but she could be any age between that and forty. She is smiling, but you do not quite believe her.

■ ■ ■

On a vacation some years ago, my husband and I visited the Mexican Marketplace in San Antonio. Almost every stall sold posters featuring some visual trickery: a lush young woman's pointy bosom becomes, when viewed from another angle, the jagged beak of a crone; as you glance back a skeleton transforms into a cowboy with a smoking gun. At the time this art seemed symbolic of San Antonio itself, its underground Riverwalk lined with tourist-filled restaurants and hotels, and its streets with empty storefronts and panhandlers. But as I reflect on my youthful writing years, these garish posters provide some metaphoric insight into my difficulty now in describing those years. There is no one self that I hold steady in my view.

■ ■ ■

What poetry did do in those days is to give me another identity, both on and off the page, and another purpose beyond burning myself at love's altar. Poetry was also my ticket out of town. My parents were trying to figure out how they might finance a boarding school education (I had been accepted to Interlochen, an arts high school in Michigan) when I announced, at fifteen, that in the fall I would be leaving high school early to go to college, having met my new school's recruiter at a writers' conference.

Antioch, a liberal arts college in Ohio, was in expansion mode and saw as part of its mission the creation of branch campuses in places where students might have little access to higher education, including the Appalachian coalfields. Antioch/Appalachia, in Beckley, West Virginia, was founded in the mid-1970s by teacher and poet, Bob Snyder. By the time I entered the fold, Antioch/Appalachia had drawn in a number of poets, both as faculty and as students. It had published two issues of a literary magazine entitled, *"What's a Nice Hillbilly Like You...?"* and had gotten a little national exposure for its efforts.

Though I had seen college as an opportunity for a fresh start, I had no expectation that I would need also to recreate

As far as I knew at that time, poetry had no accent, no dialect; it was the universal language (albeit English) of the overwrought heart.

myself as an Appalachian poet. As far as I knew at that time, poetry had no accent, no dialect; it was the universal language (albeit English) of the overwrought heart. And now here I was in the midst of a regional literary movement for which the personal lyric and I were quite ill-equipped. The writing persona I had created, heavily influenced by nineteenth century literature and 1970s female singer/songwriters, felt inappropriate among my new tribe. All around me I saw writers taking on much bigger themes—oppression, injustice, the environment, and doing so within a fairly specific cultural context, an Appalachia that I did not yet recognize as my own. For all my reading, writing and precocity, I was not an intellectual. I had no political analysis and had never known I was supposed to. I had lived through no particular hardship that I was willing to recognize as such. My best friend at college had survived the Buffalo Creek flood, a disaster caused by strip mining that decimated her small community. She wrote of being haunted by drowned faces of cousins killed in the flood. Another student wrote poems about her family of miners wounded by hard lives and capitalism. All I had to work from was my own life, and the closer I got to the truths of it, the more difficult writing became. As my college years progressed, I wrote less and less. I was a "writer," publishing and giving readings throughout the region and beyond. But I was not writing.

■ ■ ■

I left the mountains for graduate school in the city, Cincinnati, just before my twentieth birthday. Though my studies were in education rather than literature, I made connections there with several overlapping communities of writers, including those with mountain transplants like myself. Fueled by exposure to other kinds of poetry and by new sources of romantic angst (Ah, Love! Ah, Loss!) I came closest then to writing "poetry as survival," that is, poetry reaching for a depth and honesty that would allow me as writer to make sense of my own experience. But the unmaskedness terrified me; I could not sustain it. By age twenty-five, I stopped writing altogether, not long after a much revered older writer had taken me aside at the annual Appalachian Writers' Workshop to tell me that I was a good poet, and needed to be more careful; my poems revealed too much. It was not this man's well-intentioned advice that stopped my writing. He was a mirror for my own fear of writing as a form of exposure, whether to others or to my own self.

■ ■ ■

There is not all that much to say about that decade of not writing, if only because there is no written record from which to remember (re-member) it. I stayed on in Cincinnati after grad school. For a few years I thrashed with issues of identity, both the question of the relevance of my Appalachian upbringing to my life now, and whether I was still a writer although I did not, at the moment, happen to be writing. After awhile I consciously chose to let the writer identity go and attempted to kill off my old (creative, romantic, obsessive) self and make somebody new. I consciously, deliberately cut off my access to my fantasy life. I refused to dream. First, to daydream, and then without *that* slippery slope into the unconscious, I lost my ability to dream at all as, for months on end, I did not sleep, or not deeply enough to dream. My struggle with depression came to a head after yet another failed romance. I entered therapy. I eventually took a job offering programs in inner-city communities where families of other Appalachian migrants had settled. I sometimes contracted artists—writers, actors, musicians—to engage residents in using art as a tool for individual and community empowerment. I maintained close ties with my Appalachian writing community, despite my assertion that I was not a writer myself. I see now that as effectively as I cut off my identity as writer during that period, I was simultaneously working to put in place much of what I would need to reclaim it: arts, therapy, supportive peers.

■ ■ ■

No one thing brought the desire to write back into the foreground. There was, instead, a gradual opening, a heightened awareness of the world. The color of the autumn sky. An exquisite melancholy at dusk. The red clay around the roots of a plant from my mother's garden now transplanted into my own. Sometime during this period an area teenager shot and killed his family, then held his classmates hostage before his capture. There was something in that event—too terrible to imagine, much less to place myself inside that boy's despair—that caught me, that snagged on something inside me. I wanted to speak to it, but I was not writing, and did not know how.

Within a few months of allowing this longing back into my life, I joined a women's writing program which focused on providing a supportive community for women to write and share, rather than on skill-building or writing for publication. After my experience of "too much, too soon" within my earlier writing life, this was the incubator I needed; when I was ready to move into crafting and publication I sought and found additional mentors and writing communities.

This was over twenty years ago. Since this time I have also begun to serve as mentor and teacher for other writers, and to do myself what I once hired others to do—lead writing workshops in communities and schools, not just for the purpose of helping children and adults build skills in self-expression, but to allow the process of writing to deepen understanding of their own lives. As I have told my story, in poetry and prose, and heard the stories of others I have come to understand that while the details of finding, losing and rediscovering my writing voice are uniquely my own, the pattern is not. For young women writers, particularly, there is an urge toward truth-telling that is matched by an awareness of the dangers inherent in making private truths public, especially when the writer has not done the full work of processing those truths, both on and off the page. In my case, I moved early, too early I believe now, to a public identity as a writer and struggled unsuccessfully to hold all the conflicting demands; I had neither the craft nor the emotional maturity for poetry to be a tool for my survival, nor the guidance from others who could help me use it as such. I came back to writing in my thirties ready, then, to carry on with the work and determined to understand my own history in order not to repeat it. This determination fuels my both my writing and my teaching. I teach from a desire to provide others the support I had needed long before I found it. I teach in order to stay connected to that tender balance of fear and fortitude that allows—necessitates—the telling of our truths. This, then, is what I believe about the teaching and writing of poetry, and why I do both:

1. The main purpose of writing is to go deeper into the truth of our own lives. Not doing this will eventually destroy our abilities to write.

2. Form will follow function; if we follow the impulse to tell the truth to the extent of our abilities, then our abilities will stretch to create the best container for that truth.

3. Each writer's first audience is herself. If we are going to write, then we need to write first to satisfy our impulse toward illumination of the self and the world around us.[4]

4 Ammons, A.R. "Poetics" in *Collected Poems*, 1951-1971. (New York: W. W. Norton & Company, 2001).

4. If a writer chooses to go beyond this audience, then her job is to bring those truths to the page in such a way that they are no longer hers, but ours. Again, form will follow function—all the various tropes and techniques are to serve this purpose.

5. Community can enhance this process; it can also hinder it. The clearer we become about what we and our writing need from others, the more likely we are to get it.

6. Writing is not therapy. Therapy is therapy. But they share a common denominator, of deep truth telling, and both draw from the wells fed by preconscious and unconscious sources; childhood, family, dreams. And like prayer and other spiritual practices, they require a certain amount of faith in the process itself. ■

KINPEOPLE

Like all men bleeding out
on the battlefield, he wants his mother.
He wants Sunday dinner, the farm-fresh girl
creamy and veined as bluejohn, the calves'
brains she scrambled with eggs of a morning.

In his fog of confusion,
my father wants her shyness, coming
home to simpler times before the war,
the strawberry blond who covered
her mouth when she laughed.

Some days I tell him
she's frying those apples he loves, others
I say she's thirty years gone. He searches
among the casualties, the unexploded
shells, limbs cockeyed as ragdolls
on the beachhead.

He leans in closer:
Are you my kinpeople? Yes, I am, I say.
I'm your kinpeople. Then he searches on
for flares of the once known, for Annie Louise
pouring tea in the Fostoria, not slicing
the roast till he sits. He picks through
bloodied rocks for shards of her name.

LINDA PARSONS

CAVE COUNTRY

Consider the sinkhole formation, the sudden black dot
emerging from green pasture, growing, eating, swallowing.
Cool air spills from below, bends the scorched grass.

Consider the properties of this formation—the presence
of dark, the absence of light, moist ground beneath
the dry surface—a lost trust that the earth

will continue to hold. Consider how the world you know
is cut in two. As you descend, first the feet and then
the legs disappear, then the hips and then the head.

But, you protest, you are still present. The heart's evidence
taps against the temple, the way it does when tense.
Consider everything you know of burial

of underworlds, all the stories of black and white.
Consider whether you've changed one damn bit,
not being seen but felt, sometimes heard.

Consider the meaning of darkness without
the mythologies of hell, that place where what
you thought was true, has started to shift.

D.A. GRAY

ONE EVENING IN EARLY SPRING

The visible remains of another day are evident as grey light
above treetops. Shadows have swallowed the back yard;
our white salamander friend arrives, climbing to the soffit,
upside down. A feral cat's outline emerges against the sky
on the corner fence post. The small gods are waking.

An owl, known only by the breeze of its wings, passes
and an opossum ambles through a patch of windowlight.
We step out the back door, no flashlight, silent in our deck
chairs at the edge of the porch. The kids race into the dark,
position betrayed only by the sound of laughter. I, having slowed
with age, close my eyes, listening for evidence: the cat racing
away, the neighbor dog barking, followed by another dog
in the distance. This way we map our known world.
The kids ask us to come play and so we move into the night.
In time our eyes adjust. Outside the electric light's radius
we begin to see it, the not being alone, the way bodies
under the moon begin to illuminate, the ivy, the sharp grass blades—

until a siren splinters the air, and red light blinds us all.

D.A. GRAY

BOOK REVIEW

Robert Gipe. *Weedeater*. Athens, Oh.: Ohio University Press, 2018. 250 pages. Hardcover. $27.95.

Reviewed by Leah Hampton

Dawn Jewell is back. Robert Gipe's second novel, a sequel to the much-loved *Trampoline*, revisits our favorite citizens of Canard County, Kentucky. While *Weedeater* is a standalone work, those who have not yet read Gipe's first book should be advised that they are definitely missing out, and some *Trampoline* spoilers follow.

Weedeater takes place six years after the close of the previous novel, at the dawn of the opioid crisis. Dawn Jewell is now married to the bumbling, affectionate Willett Bilson, and she has a young daughter, Nicolette, who just might be a prodigy. Also returning are Dawn's drug-addicted momma and fiery mamaw, along with Aunt June, uncle Hubert, and other familiar faces. New to the

Canard roster is the titular character, Weedeater, aka Gene, whose voice fills up half the pages of the novel. Narrated entirely in first person, the story bounces between Gene's laconic, endearing account of his hopeless love for Aunt June, and Dawn's caustic, searching wit.

The action centers around Aunt June's return to Canard County and her plans to teach a class at the local community college, build a public art installation, and generally tidy up after her sister and the Jewell clan. Aunt June "loves a project," and Dawn and Gene take turns in that role narrating her efforts, along with recounting their own tribulations. Dawn's mother is spiraling further into her addiction while Hubert, Mamaw, and Dawn's brother Albert are all still making messes. Meanwhile, Dawn is sorting out her own identity as a mother and wife. Gene seems most precarious of all as he reluctantly enmeshes himself in June's family dramas, barely hanging on to his home and heart on every page.

Weedeater engages with many of the same tensions as its predecessor, and shows us how the social problems in Canard County have complicated in the ensuing years. Yet this is a slimmer volume than *Trampoline,* less dense in terms of plot and narrative. Perhaps because of the dual narrators, or because we already know most characters' back stories, *Weedeater*'s plot unfolds easily and gracefully, despite its tough subject matter. Gipe keeps the action moving with plenty of fist fights, snappy dialogue, and even a little spelunking. The author's exceptional humor also works brilliantly here, and the book is downright uproarious without ever mocking its subjects. Only Gipe can make powerful trouble feel like such a treat.

We are also treated once again to a rich array of Gipe's embedded illustrations. *Weedeater* is officially termed "an illustrated novel," and this concept feels just as fresh as it did in the first book. Gipe weaves between text and visual elements unlike any other writer in the region—or in contemporary literary fiction, for that matter. The art here is well wrought and deceptively simple. Each choice Gipe makes—with placement, captions, and movement—reinforces the shadows and pathos of these characters. Word and image are as much in conversation in the reader's head as they are on the page. Reading *Weedeater* is not like reading a story, nor is it like reading a comic or graphic novel. The experience is something else entirely, challenging our expectations for metaphor and Appalachian representation, constantly forcing us to re-see, to re-think a moment, a scene, a feeling. Some of the pictures are pretty hilarious, too.

Despite all these familiar elements, *Weedeater* does not rely too heavily on its predecessor. This is a new story, and Gipe takes us in a very different direction throughout. On the surface, the plot is entirely original and self contained. Unlike *Trampoline,* this second novel is less about activism and more about aftermath. All the characters, even the most sympathetic ones, are beginning to reap consequences for their actions, and Gipe shows us the nuances of people wrestling with accumulating circumstance.

Dig a little deeper, and we also find that Gipe's writing style has matured and taken on more complexity. While there is no shortage of heartbreaking passages in *Trampoline,* in *Weedeater* the writing is even clearer and closer to the heart. Dawn Jewell is a grown woman now. She has a child to think about, along with added years of stress and strife; in this book we see her balancing her keen, ragged emotions ever more unsteadily. All the Jewells, in fact, have more facets here. And through Gene's voice, we access a pure, resonant longing that anyone who loves our region will recognize. In *Trampoline* it was eastern Kentucky—the land itself—that was naked, vulnerable, threatened. Here the vulnerability has taken deeper root in her people.

The language of *Weedeater* is stronger, more plaintive, and more honest, perhaps because its landscape is more interior, more intimate. Gene's tender masculinity helps us understand and value the softness we often surrender all too easily during difficult times. Unlike Dawn, who does not allow herself any tenderness, and who does not feel safe caring for anybody, Gene shows us true love, raw, pure, and often unreasonable. Love like that struggles to survive in places like Canard County, and the book ends with a clue about the places such love can lead, leaving the reader full of ideas and questions for the next book in the series.

The lesson of *Weedeater*, Gipe seems to be telling us, is that there is great power in vulnerability. We, as individuals and as citizens of this region, should all be turning towards our longing, and towards the people who activate that longing, rather than turning away from them. ■

WILLOW

Who will make
Your long bed,
Smooth your grass quilt,
fluff your stone pillow?

Who will tuck
the dry dirt
under your chin,
sing in my place
in the songless night
under bright dots of light
in the dark, curved sky,
sing Willow?

Sing Willow.

Sing Willow.

MARY ELLEN MILLER

CONTRIBUTORS

D.A. Gray is the author of one previous collection of poems, *Overwatch* (Grey Sparrow Press, 2011). His poetry has appeared in *The Sewanee Review, Appalachian Heritage, Kentucky Review, The Good Men Project, Still: The Journal, War, Literature and the Arts* among many other journals. Gray recently completed his graduate work at The Sewanee School of Letters and at Texas A&M-Central Texas.

Leah Hampton is a fiction fellow at the Michener Center for Writers. Her work has appeared in *storySouth, Still: The Journal, North Carolina Literary Review,* and elsewhere. She lives in Haywood County, North Carolina.

Pauletta Hansel is the author of six poetry collections, including *Palindrome* (Dos Madres Press, 2017), written in response to her mother's dementia. Hansel is Cincinnati's first Poet Laureate (2016-2018) and is co-editor of *Pine Mountain Sand & Gravel,* the literary publication of Southern Appalachian Writers Cooperative.

A native of upper East Tennessee, **Jane Hicks** is an award-winning poet and quilter. She is the author of two poetry collections: *Blood and Bone Remember* and *Driving with the Dead.* Her poetry has appeared in journals and numerous anthologies, and her "literary quilts" illustrate the works of playwright Jo Carson and novelists Sharyn McCrumb and Silas House.

Mary Hostetter's recent writing has appeared in *Prime Number, The Gettysburg Review* and the *New York Times,* as Modern Love Essay. She has taken writing classes at the University of Virginia and at WriterHouse in Charlottesville, and has been awarded several fellowships to Virginia Center for the Creative Arts.

Silas House is the nationally best-selling author of five novels. He is a frequent contributor to the *New York Times* and he currently serves as the NEH Chair at Berea College and on the fiction faculty at Spalding University's MFA in Writing program. His latest novel, *Southernmost,* will be published in June 2018.

Rebecca Gayle Howell is the author of *American Purgatory* and *Render /An Apocalypse*. Her awards include fellowships from the Fine Arts Work Center and the Carson McCullers Center, as well as a Pushcart Prize. Howell is the James Still Writer-in-Residence at the Hindman Settlement School in Knott County, Kentucky, and the poetry editor for *Oxford American*.

A Ph.D. student in creative writing at Georgia State University, **Joshua Lee Martin** has been published in *The Cumberland River Review, decomP, The Soundings Review, Town Creek Poetry The Kentucky Review, Iodine Poetry Journal, The San Pedro River Review, The Concho River Review*, and elsewhere. He recently was a finalist in the 2016 Nazim Hikmet Poetry Competition, and his chapbook, *Passing Through Meat Camp*, was a finalist in the 2015 Jacar Press Chapbook Competition.

Jake Maynard is a thirty-year-old recent graduate of the MFA program at West Virginia University. A former social worker, his writing appears in recent or forthcoming issues of *River Teeth, Carolina Quarterly*, and *Fugue*.

Mary Ellen Miller has been a professor of English at Western Kentucky University for fifty-four years, co-founding the Center for Robert Penn Warren Studies. The author of *The Poet's Wife Speaks*, she also co-edited (with Morris Grubbs) *Every Leaf a Mirror: A Jim Wayne Miller Reader*, a multi-genre anthology compiling the work of her late husband. A native of Carter County, Kentucky, she graduated from Berea College with a degree in English.

Lisa J. Parker is the author of the 2010 Weatherford Award-winning book *This Gone Place* and her work has appeared in numerous literary magazines and anthologies. She received her MFA in Creative Writing from Pennsylvania State University, and has been awareded the Randall Jarrell Prize In Poetry, the National Allen Tate Memorial Prize In Poetry, and an Academy of American Poets Prize.

Linda Parsons is a poet and playwright. She is the reviews editor for *Pine Mountain Sand & Gravel* and served as poetry editor of *Now & Then* magazine for many years. Her work has appeared in such journals as *The Georgia Review, One, Iowa Review, Prairie Schooner,*

Southern Poetry Review, Shenandoah, Writers Resist, in Ted Kooser's column *American Life in Poetry,* and in numerous anthologies. *This Shaky Earth* is her fourth poetry collection.

Jon Sealy is the author of *The Whiskey Baron.* His stories have also appeared in *The South Carolina Review, The Normal School, PANK,* and *The Sun.* He lives in Richmond, Virginia.

Stephanie Strasburg is based in Pittsburgh and works as a staff photographer for the *Pittsburgh Post-Gazette.* She is drawn to document the changing landscape, economy, and culture of the Rust Belt, returning often with her camera to the mill towns of the Mon Valley outside of Pittsburgh. Her work has appeared in the *New York Times, The Wall Street Journal, USA Today, Reuters, Science Magazine, STAT News, Vox.com,* and other outlets.

Lyrae Van Clief-Stefanon is the author of *Open Interval,* a 2009 National Book Award finalist, and *Black Swan,* winner of the 2001 Cave Canem Poetry Prize, as well as *Poems in Conversation and a Conversation,* a chapbook collaboration with Elizabeth Alexander. She is currently at work on *The Coal Tar Colors,* her third poetry collection, and *Purchase,* a collection of essays. She teaches at Cornell University in Ithaca, New York.